Praise for
BUILDING SOCIAL BUSINESS

"In nine short, well-written chapters, Yunus provides genuine insight into global poverty and a unique perspective on the ways in which social businesses can coexist with traditional businesses to alleviate poverty and improve the lives of the world's citizens."
—*CHOICE*

"Giving poor people the resources to help themselves, Dr. Yunus has offered these individuals something more valuable than a plate of food, namely, security in its basic form. . . . Dr. Yunus has invoked a new basis for capitalism whereby social business has the potential to change the failed promise of free-market enterprise."
—*Sacramento Book Review*

"I found much to admire here and in the man, whose work I have long respected. The book is a refreshingly easy read. . . . [Yunus] fills his book with practical examples, tactics, ideas, and insights."
—*Stanford Social Innovation Review*

"[A] reminder that capitalism can take kindlier forms: Microfinance pioneer Yunus explains how he believes social enterprise can redeem what he regards as the failed promise of free markets."
—*The Spectator*

"There are times when Professor Yunus' aims for Glasgow sound like something out of the Conservative's 'Big Society' pitch. His latest book, *Building Social Business*, is 300 pages of Big Society pleading for people to go out there and create businesses which generate cash and contribute to the greater good at the same time."
—*The Independent*

"'Social business is about joy,' says Yunus. Indeed, and the book itself is joy to read. In modest prose, Yunus tells of undertakings that instill hope. He also gives a lot of ideas, along with nuts-and-bolts practical advice for people who are ready to take the plunge

into the world of social business. In the years to come, it seems certain that social business will become an integral part of our economic structure and will positively change the lives of many people."
—*Malaysia Star*

"Yunus may be an astute (social) businessman, but he also has a savvy side. He is quick to point out that working for any social business does not mean lowering one's standards, for they offer employees competitive salaries and benefits; it simply means not profiting from the poor. . . . Yunus has a Nobel Peace Prize (2006, shared with Grameen Bank) to show for his efforts, and is already playing around with the building blocks of a new poverty-free world order."
—*Daily Times* (Pakistan)

"Even a hard-core skeptic would find it difficult not to dream once the magic of Dr. Muhammad Yunus' words as presented in the book start to make sense."
—*Daily Star* (Pakistan)

"Yunus's approach is balanced and practical. There is no sermonising or the usual 'we are from the not-for-profit sector and do-gooders so we know best' approach . . . one cannot but marvel at Yunus's intense attempts to champion the cause of eradicating poverty. His is a case of a noted economist making a journey into the real world to face real problems and happily using his personal brand to strike tie-ups with leading multinationals to solve these problems. He needs to be read, understood; and he needs to be judged not only on his results, but on the sheer weight of his efforts. In India, good writing on the social sector is woefully inadequate. While high-profile outfits such as the Bill & Melinda Gates Foundation have helped raise visibility in the sector, there is still little understanding of social business. This is an excellent read in that space."
—*Business World* (India)

BUILDING
SOCIAL
BUSINESS

ALSO BY MUHAMMAD YUNUS

Banker to the Poor
Creating a World Without Poverty

BUILDING SOCIAL BUSINESS

The New Kind of Capitalism
that Serves Humanity's
Most Pressing Needs

MUHAMMAD YUNUS

with Karl Weber

PUBLICAFFAIRS
New York

To all those who are ready to
dedicate themselves to change the world

Book Design by Brent Wilcox

The Library of Congress has catalogued the hardcover as follows:
Yunus, Muhammad, 1940-
    Building social business : the new kind of capitalism that serves humanity's
most pressing needs / Muhammad Yunus with Karl Weber.
        p.   cm.
    Includes index.
    ISBN 978-1-58648-824-6 (hardcover)
    1. Social responsibility of business.   2. Social entrepreneurship.
3. Capitalism—Moral and ethical aspects.   I. Weber, Karl, 1953-   II. Title.
HD60.Y85 2010
658.4'07—dc22
                                                        2010002857

Paperback ISBN: 978-1-58648-956-4
e-book ISBN: 978-1-58648-863-5
LSC-C
11

CONTENTS

Social Business— From Dream to Reality

Beginning with a Tiny Step

I first got involved in the poverty problem as an academician, and then personally, almost by accident. I got involved because poverty was all around me in Bangladesh. In particular, the famine of 1974 pushed me out of the university campus and forced me to become a social activist in addition to being a teacher.

This is a common experience, of course. In disaster situations, most of us without hesitation take up the social roles demanded by human compassion. But in my case what began in a time of crisis became a lifelong calling. I gave up my academic position and founded a bank— a bank for the poor.

It was the first step in a journey that continues to this day. The latest stage in that journey, as I'll explain in this book, is creating and realizing an idea for a new form of capitalism and a new kind of enterprise based on the selflessness of people, which I call social business. It's a kind of business dedicated to solving social, economic, and environmental problems that have long plagued humankind—hunger, homelessness, disease, pollution, ignorance.

Back in the early seventies, the newly independent country of Bangladesh was in a terrible state. The aftermath of our War of Liberation—

with the destruction caused by the Pakistani army—combined with floods, droughts, and monsoons to create a desperate situation for millions of people. Then came the famine. I found it increasingly difficult to teach elegant theories of economics in the classroom while a terrible famine was raging outside. Suddenly I felt the emptiness of traditional economic concepts in the face of crushing hunger and poverty. I realized that I had to be with the distressed people of Jobra, the neighboring village just outside of Chittagong University, and somehow find something to do for them. All that I hoped to do was make myself useful to at least one person per day.

In trying to discover what I could do to help, I learned many things about Jobra, about the poor people who lived there, and about their helplessness. I came face to face with the struggle of the poor to find the tiniest amounts of money needed to support their efforts to eke out a living.

In particular, I was shocked to meet a woman who had borrowed just 5 taka (the equivalent of around 7 cents in U.S. currency) from a moneylender and trader. She needed this small amount of money to buy bamboo, from which she crafted stools to sell. The interest rate on such loans was very high—as much as 10 percent per week. But still worse was the special condition imposed on the loan: She would have to sell all her products to the moneylender at a price he would determine.

That 5-taka loan transformed her into a virtual slave. No matter how hard she might work, she and her family could never escape from poverty.

To understand the scope of this moneylending practice in the village, I made a list of the people who had borrowed from the moneylenders. When my list was complete, it had forty-two names. These people had borrowed a total of 856 taka from the moneylenders— roughly U.S. $27 at then-current exchange rates. It seemed absurd that such a small amount of money should have created so much misery!

To free these forty-two people from the clutches of the moneylenders, I reached into my own pocket and gave them the money to repay the loans. The excitement that was created in the village by this small action touched me deeply. I thought, "If this little action makes so many people so happy, why shouldn't I do more of this?"

That's what I have been trying to do ever since.

The first thing I did was to try to persuade the bank located in the university campus to lend money to the poor. But the bank manager refused. He said, "The poor do not qualify to receive loans from the bank—they are not creditworthy." I argued with him with no result. I met with senior banking officials at various levels to see if I could find someone who would be willing to open the doors of the bank to the poor. This went on for several months, but I couldn't change their minds.

Finally, I came up with an idea. I offered to become a guarantor for loans to the poor. After much hesitation, the bank agreed to accept this proposal. By the middle of 1976, I started giving out loans to the village poor, signing all the papers the bank gave me to guarantee the loans personally and acting as a kind of informal banker on my own. I wanted to make sure that the poor borrowers would find it easy to pay back the loans, so I came up with simple rules, such as having people repay their loans in small weekly amounts, and having the bank officer visit the villagers rather than making the villagers visit the bank. These ideas worked. People paid back the loans on time, every time.

It seemed to me that lending money to the poor was not as difficult as was generally imagined. It even appeared to me that serving their financial needs might be a viable business. You'd think a smart banker would be able to recognize this opportunity quicker than a mere economics professor with no banking experience. But no. I kept confronting difficulties in trying to expand the program through existing banks.

Finally, with no other option, I decided to create a separate bank for the poor. It was a long, arduous process. But with the support of the then-finance minister of Bangladesh, I succeeded in creating a new bank, a bank dedicated to serve the poor. We called it Grameen Bank—or "village bank," in the Bengali language.

Today, Grameen Bank is a nationwide bank serving the poor in every single village of Bangladesh. Of its 8 million borrowers, 97 percent are women. Early in the history of the bank, we deliberately decided to focus on lending to women—initially as a protest against the practice of conventional banks, which refused to lend money to women even if they belonged to a high income bracket. We also saw that women in Bangladesh had the talent and skill to become income-earners. Our initial goal was to make sure we had both men and women borrowers in even numbers. But soon we discovered, through experience, that female borrowers brought much more benefit to their families than male borrowers. Children immediately benefited from the income of their mothers. Women had more drive to overcome poverty. Lending to women in the poor villages of Bangladesh, we realized, was a powerful way to combat poverty for the entire society.

Grameen Bank is unusual in other ways. It is actually owned by the borrowers, who in their capacity as shareholders elect nine of the thirteen members of the board of directors. Grameen Bank lends out over $100 million a month in collateral-free loans averaging about $200. The repayment rate on loans remains very high, about 98 percent, despite the fact that Grameen Bank focuses on the poorest people—those whom conventional banks still consider non-creditworthy.

Grameen Bank even lends money to beggars. They use the loans to enter the business of selling goods—toys, household items, foodstuffs—from door to door, along with begging door to door. Contrary to some people's expectation, beggars like the idea of supporting themselves through sales rather than relying on charity. We now have over 100,000 beggars in this program. During the four years since this program was launched, over 18,000 have quit begging. Most of the beggars are now on their second and third loans.

Grameen Bank also encourages children of its borrowers to go to school, offering affordable loans for them to pursue higher education.

More than 50,000 students are currently pursuing their education in medical schools, engineering schools, and universities with financing from Grameen Bank.

We encourage these young people to pledge that they will never enter the job market to seek jobs from anybody. They'll be job givers, not job seekers. We explain to them, "Your mothers own a big bank, Grameen Bank. It has plenty of money to finance any enterprise you may wish to float, so why waste time looking for a job working for someone else? Instead, be an employer rather than an employee." Grameen Bank is in the business of encouraging entrepreneurship and self-reliance among the people of Bangladesh—not dependence.

Grameen Bank is financially self-reliant. All of its funds come from deposits. More than half of the deposits come from the borrowers themselves, who are required to save a little bit every week. They have a collective savings balance of over half a billion U.S. dollars.

All of this would be an impressive enough achievement based on the tiny spark that started it all—that $27 worth of loans that I repaid for the poor people of Jobra. But the work of Grameen Bank in Bangladesh has turned out to be just the beginning.

Today the idea of small, collateral-free loans for poor women, known as "microcredit" or "microfinance," has spread around the world. There are now Grameen-type programs in almost every country in the world. We even run a program named Grameen America in New York City. Its first branch was opened in Queens, New York, in 2008 to provide small collateral-free loans (averaging $1500) to local women to start modest businesses or expand their existing businesses. Most of them are single mothers struggling to make a living with dignity.

Grameen America is now branching out to new locations in Brooklyn, New York, Omaha, Nebraska, and San Francisco, California. Its success demonstrates that even in the richest country in the world with the most sophisticated banking system, there is a huge need for banks dedicated to serving the unserved and underserved millions.

Why do I attach such importance to the idea of providing banking services to the poor? Partly, of course, because of the way I stumbled upon the role of the exploitative moneylenders in trapping people in poverty. But it's also because I have become increasingly convinced that poverty is *not* created by poor people themselves.

When I meet Grameen Bank borrowers, I often meet mother-daughter and mother-son pairs in which the mother is totally illiterate, while the daughter or son is a medical doctor or an engineer. A thought always flashes through my mind: This mother could have been a doctor or an engineer, too. She has the same capability as her daughter or son. The only reason she could not unleash her potential is that the society never gave her the chance. She could not even go to school to learn the alphabet.

The more time you spend among poor people, the more you become convinced that poverty is not the result of any incapacity on the part of the poor. Poverty is not created by poor people. It is created by the system we have built, the institutions we have designed, and the concepts we have formulated.

Poverty is created by deficiencies in the institutions we have built—for example, financial institutions. These banks refuse to provide financial services to nearly two-thirds of the world's population. For generations they claimed it could not be done, and everybody accepted that explanation. This allowed loan sharks to thrive all over the world. Grameen Bank questioned this assumption and demonstrated that lending money to the poorest is not only possible but profitable.

During the global financial crisis that began in 2008, the falsity of the old assumptions became even more visible. While big conventional banks with all their collateral were collapsing, around the world microcredit programs, which do not depend on collateral, continued to be as strong as ever. Will this demonstration make the mainstream financial institutions change their minds about their traditional definition of creditworthiness? Will they finally open their doors to the poor?

I am quite serious about this question (although I know all too well what the likely answer is). When a crisis is at its deepest, it can offer a huge opportunity. When things fall apart, we can redesign, recast, and rebuild. We should not miss this opportunity to convert our financial institutions into inclusive institutions. Nobody should be refused access to financial services. Because these services are so vital for people's self-realization, I strongly feel that credit should be given the status of a human right.

That poverty is created not by poor people but by their circumstances tells us something else important—something about the potential of human beings themselves.

Every human being is born into this world fully equipped not only to take care of himself or herself, but also to contribute to the well-being of the world as a whole. Some get the chance to explore their potential, but many others never get the chance to unwrap the wonderful gifts they were born with. They die with those gifts unexplored, and the world remains deprived of their contribution.

Grameen has given me an unshakeable faith in human creativity and the firm belief that human beings are not born to suffer the misery of hunger and poverty. Poverty is an artificial, external imposition on a person. And since it is external, it can be removed.

We can create a poverty-free world if we redesign our system to take out its gross flaws which create poverty. We can create a world in which the only place you would be able to see poverty is in poverty museums. Someday, schoolchildren will be taken to visit these poverty museums. They will be horrified to see the misery and indignity that innumerable people had to go through for no fault of their own. They will blame their ancestors for tolerating this inhuman condition for so long—and rightly so.

To me, poor people are like bonsai trees. When you plant the best seed from the tallest tree in a tiny flowerpot, you get a replica of the tallest tree, only inches tall. There is nothing wrong with the seed you planted; only the soil base that you gave it is inadequate. Poor people are bonsai people. There is nothing wrong with their seeds, but society never gave them the proper base to grow in. All it takes to get poor people out of poverty is for us to create an enabling environment for them. Once the poor can unleash their energy and creativity, poverty will disappear very quickly.

The Concept of Social Business

I took my first step in the direction of helping poor people in the mid-seventies. While poverty has remained my main concern since then, I have moved on to other issues because I've found them very relevant to my main concern. Over time I've become involved in agriculture, livestock, fisheries, renewable energy, information technology, education, health, hand-loom textiles, employment services, and many similar areas and sub-areas under them. Each one, I thought, could help overcome poverty if designed in the right way. For each sector or subsector I created a company to see whether I could address the problem of poverty in a sustainable way. Poverty is a state of living. It has many facets. It has to be approached from many directions, and no approach is insignificant.

While trying out all these approaches, I saw myself moving from one level to another level of my conceptual framework. I moved from microcredit to a much broader concept, which neatly includes microcredit itself. This new concept will bring a fundamental change in the architecture of our capitalist economy by bringing it closer to a complete and satisfactory framework, freeing it from the basic flaws which lead to poverty and other social and environmental ills. This is the concept of *social business*, which is the subject of this book.

Let me return for a moment to the financial crisis of 2008–2009. Unfortunately, media coverage gives the impression that once we fix this crisis, all our troubles will be over: The economy will start to grow again, and we can quickly and comfortably return to "business as usual."

But even if it were desirable, business as usual is not really a viable option. We forget that the financial crisis is only one of several crises threatening humankind. We are also suffering a global food crisis, an energy crisis, an environmental crisis, a healthcare crisis, and the continuing social and economic crisis of massive worldwide poverty. These crises are as important as the financial one, although they have not received as much attention.

Furthermore, the media coverage may give the impression that these are disconnected crises that are taking place simultaneously, just by accident. That's not true at all. In fact, these crises grow from the same root—a fundamental flaw in our theoretical construct of capitalism.

The biggest flaw in our existing theory of capitalism lies in its misrepresentation of human nature. In the present interpretation of capitalism, human beings engaged in business are portrayed as one-dimensional beings whose only mission is to maximize profit. Humans supposedly pursue this economic goal in a single-minded fashion.

This is a badly distorted picture of a human being. As even a moment's reflection suggests, human beings are not money-making robots. The essential fact about humans is that they are multidimensional beings. Their happiness comes from many sources, not just from making money.

And yet economists have built their whole theory of business on the assumption that human beings do nothing in their economic lives besides pursue selfish interests. The theory concludes that the optimal result for society will occur when each individual's search for selfish benefit is given free rein. This interpretation of human beings denies any role to other aspects of life—political, social, emotional, spiritual, environmental, and so on.

No doubt humans are selfish beings, but they are selfless beings, too. Both these qualities coexist in all human beings. Self-interest and the pursuit of profit explain many of our actions, but many others make no sense when viewed through this distorting lens. If the profit motive alone controlled all of human behavior, the only existing institutions would be ones designed to generate maximum individual wealth. There would be no churches or mosques or synagogues, no schools, no art museums, no public parks or health clinics or community centers. (After all, institutions like these don't make anyone into a tycoon!) There would be no charities, foundations, or nonprofit organizations.

Obviously human beings are driven by selfless motivations as well. The existence of countless charitable institutions supported by personal generosity demonstrates this. (It is true that in many countries donors to charity receive tax benefits for their gifts. But these tax breaks only repay a portion of the money donated. An altruistic motivation is still required to make charity possible.) And yet this selfless dimension has no role in economics.

This distorted view of human nature is the fatal flaw that makes our economic thinking incomplete and inaccurate. Over time, it has helped to create the multiple crises we face today. Our government regulations, our educational systems, our social structures are all based on the assumption that only selfish motivations are "real" and deserve attention. As a result, we invest vast amounts of time, energy, money, and other resources in developing and supporting for-profit businesses. We assume that for-profit businesses are the chief source of human creativity and the only way to address society's problems. And even as our problems get worse, we fail to question the underlying assumptions that helped create those problems in the first place.

Once we recognize this flaw in our theoretical structure, the solution is obvious. We must replace the one-dimensional person in economic theory with a multidimensional person—a person who has both selfish and selfless interests at the same time.

When we do this, our picture of the business world immediately changes. We see the need for *two* kinds of businesses: one for personal gain, another dedicated to helping others. In one kind of business, the objective is to maximize profits for the owners with little or no consideration for others. (In fact, in the pursuit of maximum profit, many people do not mind even harming people's lives knowingly.) In the other kind of business, everything is for the benefit of others and nothing is for the owners—except the pleasure of serving humanity. The second kind of business, built on the selfless part of human nature, I have named *social business*. This is what our economic theory has been lacking.

In a social business an investor aims to help others without making any financial gain himself. The social business is a business because it must be self-sustaining—that is, it generates enough income to cover its own costs. Part of the economic surplus the social business creates is invested in expanding the business, and a part is kept in reserve to cover uncertainties. Thus, the social business might be described as a "non-loss, non-dividend company," dedicated entirely to achieving a social goal.

We can think about a social business as a selfless business whose purpose is to bring an end to a social problem. In this kind of business, the company makes a profit—but no one takes the profit. Because the company is dedicated entirely to the social cause, the whole idea of making personal profit is removed from this business. The owner can take back over a period of time only the amount invested.

Will anybody in the real world be interested in creating businesses with selfless objectives? Where would the money for social business come from?

Real human beings that all of us know will be delighted to create businesses for selfless purposes. The only thing we'll have to do is to free them from the mindset that puts profit-making at the heart of every business, an idea that we imposed on them through our flawed economic theory.

You might wonder, where will the money come from to create a business that has no intention of generating a profit? The answer is not as mysterious as you might assume. One source is the money that currently goes to support philanthropy. Think of the great foundations as well as the non-profit organizations that flourish thanks to the generosity of millions of donors, large and small. In the United States alone, the annual revenues of non-profit organizations in one recent year amounted to over $1.1 trillion!

As this number shows, people are happy to give money from their pockets to support organizations that they believe are making the world a better place. If people can see that social business can do a better job of achieving the same goals, why wouldn't they gladly shift more and more of that charitable money into funding social businesses?

Besides wealthy philanthropists—the Bill Gateses and Warren Buffetts of the world—many other people will invest in social businesses just to share the joy of making a difference in other people's lives. People will give not only money but also their creativity, networking skills, technological prowess, life experience, and other resources to create social businesses that can change the world.

Once the idea of social business becomes known, many will divert some of their money from profit-making businesses to social businesses. That will be another source of funds for social business. Some of the government money that is traditionally spent on social programs will be used on social business. Social responsibility funds established by profit-making companies can also be available for social businesses.

Once our economic theory adjusts to the multidimensional reality of human nature, students will learn in their schools and colleges that there are two kinds of businesses: traditional money-making businesses and social businesses. As they grow up, they'll think about what kind of company they will invest in and what kind of company they will work for. And many young people who dream of a better world will think about what kind of social business they would like to create. When they are still in school, young people may start designing social businesses and even launch social businesses individually or collectively to express their creative talents in changing the world.

Not a Dream, but a Reality

Like any new idea, the concept of social business needs practical demonstration. So I have started creating social businesses in Bangladesh.

Some of them became well-known because they were created as joint ventures between Grameen companies and world-renowned multinational companies. The first such joint venture was created in 2005 in partnership with the French dairy company Danone (best known in the United States for its Dannon yogurt) and is aimed at reducing malnutrition among the children of Bangladesh. Grameen Danone produces a delicious yogurt for children and sells it at a price the poor can afford. This yogurt is fortified with all the micronutrients that are missing in the children's ordinary diet: iron, zinc, iodine, and so on. If a child eats two cups of yogurt a week over eight to nine months, he or she gets all the needed micronutrients and becomes a healthy, playful child.

As a social business, Grameen Danone follows the basic principle that it must be self-sustaining, and the owners must remain committed to never take any dividend beyond the return of the original amount they invested. The company's success is judged each year not by the amount of profit generated, but by the number of children who escape malnutrition in that particular year.

I told the story of the founding of Grameen Danone in my last book, *Creating a World Without Poverty*, and later in these pages, I'll provide an update. As you'll see, it has been an interesting learning experience that offers many lessons about how to start and develop a successful social business.

More important, Grameen Danone has served as a role model, attracting attention around the world. Many other big companies are now approaching the Grameen organization to create joint social businesses. They want to join forces with Grameen to make sure it is done the right way, and they know we originated this new concept. Once they become experienced in social business, they will take the concept wherever the need exists.

Our joint social business with Veolia, a large French water company, is called the Grameen Veolia Water Company, created to bring safe drinking water to the villages of Bangladesh where arsenic contamination is a huge problem. Villagers buy water from the company at an affordable price instead of drinking contaminated water. Over time, we'll measure the impact of the improved water supply on the health of the local people.

Another large corporation, BASF of Germany, has signed a joint venture agreement with Grameen to produce chemically treated mosquito nets in Bangladesh. When these nets are draped over beds, they provide sleepers with protection from mosquito-borne diseases such as malaria. The BASF Grameen joint venture will produce and sell these mosquito nets as cheaply as possible to make the benefits affordable to the poor.

Our joint venture with Intel Corporation, Grameen Intel, aims at using information and communication technology to help solve the problems of the rural poor—for example, by providing healthcare in villages of the developing world where doctors and nurses are scarce and medical clinics are few. As I'll explain later in this book, the goal is to create exciting new technologies that can bring the most advanced healthcare concepts within the reach of poor villagers—and then to create a cadre of small-scale entrepreneurs who will deliver these vital services in an economically sustainable fashion.

Our joint venture with adidas aims at producing affordable shoes for the lowest income people. The goal of Grameen adidas is to make sure that no one, child or adult, goes without shoes. Of course, it's more pleasant and comfortable to walk on dusty roads with shoes on your feet, but at bottom, this is a health intervention to make sure that people in rural areas, particularly children, do not have to suffer from parasitic diseases that can be transmitted through walking barefoot. Adidas is working with Grameen to bring these benefits to the poorest people of the developing world using an economically viable social business model.

Another German company, Otto GmbH, a global leader in the mail-order business, is eager to start a social business that produces textiles and garments for export from South Asia into the developed world. Otto Grameen is planning to set up a garment factory in Bangladesh that will make a special effort to employ people who are often treated as economically marginal, including single parent women and the disabled. The profits will be used to improve the quality of life for the employees, their children, and the poor of the neighborhood.

As these examples show, social business is not just a pleasant idea. It is a reality, one that is already beginning to make positive changes in people's lives as well as attracting serious interest from some of the world's most advanced corporations.

Many more social businesses are on the way. One attractive area will be in creating jobs in special locations or for particularly disadvantaged people. Since a social business operates free from the pressure of earning profit for the owners, the scope of investment opportunities is much greater than with profit-maximizing companies. Before a profit-maximizing company decides to make an investment, it has to be assured of a predetermined minimum return on investment, say 25 percent. It will not proceed with the investment if this return is not available because it has other investment opportunities which will bring that kind of return. Since the investor is a profit-seeker, he will be driven to projects by the size of profit.

But the investment decision made by a social business is not based on the potential profit. It is based on the social cause. If that cause happens to be creating employment, it will go ahead if it is satisfied that the business can sustain itself. This gives social business enormous power in creating jobs. It can even invest in projects where the return on investment is near zero, and in the process open up job opportunities for many people. In a purely profit-making business world, these jobs would never be created. How unfortunate!

Healthcare is another high-potential area for social business. Public delivery of healthcare in many countries is inefficient and often fails to reach the people who need it most. Private healthcare caters mainly to the needs of high-income people. The big empty space between the two can be filled by social businesses.

In Bangladesh, the Grameen Healthcare company is developing a prototype of health management centers in the villages that will keep healthy people healthy by concentrating on prevention and offering diagnostic and health check-up services, health insurance, education in health practices and nutrition, and so on. Grameen Healthcare is trying to take advantage of the near-universal availability of mobile phones and is working with leading manufacturers to design diagnostic equipment that can transmit images and data in real time to city-based health experts. By using the amazing new efficiencies that technology makes possible, I believe Grameen Healthcare can drive the costs of healthcare down so low that even the poorest village can be served while achieving the goal of economic self-sufficiency that is at the heart of social business.

Social business can also play a major role in improving the healthcare infrastructure. Grameen Healthcare is already in the process of setting up nursing colleges to train girls from Grameen Bank families as nurses. There is a large demand for qualified nurses both in Bangladesh and the rich countries. There is no reason why vast numbers of young girls should be sitting around in villages while these attractive job opportunities go unfilled. Nursing colleges run as social businesses can bridge this void.

Grameen Healthcare is also planning to set up secondary and tertiary health facilities, also designed as social businesses. (Later in this book, I'll tell the story of one such facility that is already under development, a unit for performing some of the most advanced surgical procedures in the world to cure children suffering from thalassemia, an otherwise fatal genetic disorder.) To train a new generation of doctors to staff these facilities, Grameen Healthcare plans to establish a University of Health Sciences and Technology.

Many other segments of healthcare are appropriate for building successful social businesses: nutrition, water, health insurance, health education and training, eye care, mother and child care, diagnostic services, and so on. It will take time to develop the prototypes. But once creative minds come up with the design for a social business and a prototype is developed successfully, it can be replicated endlessly.

Designing each small social business is like developing a seed. Once the seed is developed, anybody can plant it where it is needed. Since each unit is self-sustaining, funding does not become a constraint.

Among other things, social business is a way of putting today's most powerful technologies to work.

The world today is in possession of amazingly powerful technologies. They are growing very fast, becoming more powerful every day. Almost all of this technology is owned and controlled by profit-making businesses. All they use this technology for is to make more money, because that is the mandate their shareholders have given them.

Yet viewed more broadly, technology is simply a kind of vehicle. One can drive it to any desired destination. Since the present owners of technology want to travel to the peaks of profit-making, technology takes them there. If somebody else decides to use the existing technology to end poverty, it will take the owner in that direction. If another owner wants to use it to end diseases, the technology will go there. The choice is ours. The only problem is that the present theoretical framework under which capitalism operates does not give this choice. The inclusion of social business creates this choice.

One more point to ponder: There's actually no need to choose. Using technology for one purpose doesn't make it less effective for serving a different purpose. Actually, it is the other way around. The more diverse uses we make of technology, the more powerful it gets. Using technology for solving social problems will not reduce its effectiveness for making money, but rather enhance it.

The owners of social businesses can direct the power of technology to solve the growing list of social and economic problems, and get quick results. And in the process, they will generate even more technological ideas for future generations of scientists and engineers to develop. The world of social business will benefit not only the poor, but all of humanity.

Once the concept of social business becomes widely known, creative people will come forward with attractive designs for social businesses. Young people will develop business plans to address the most difficult social problems through social businesses. The good ideas, of course, will need to be funded. I am happy to say there are already initiatives in Europe and Japan to create social business funds to provide equity and loan support to social businesses.

In time, more sources of funding will be needed. Each level of government—international, national, state, and city—can create social business funds. These can encourage citizens and companies to create social businesses designed to address specific problems (unemployment, health, sanitation, pollution, old age, drugs, crime, the needs of disadvantaged groups such as the disabled, and so on). Bilateral and multilateral donors can also create social business funds. Foundations can earmark a percentage of their funds to support social businesses, and businesses can use their social responsibility budgets to fund social businesses.

Eventually we'll need to create a separate stock market to make it easy to invest in social businesses. Only social businesses will be listed in this social stock market, and investors will know right from the beginning that they'll never receive any dividends from this market. Their motivation will be to enjoy the pride and pleasure of helping to solve difficult social problems.

Social business gives everybody the opportunity to participate in creating the kind of world we all want to see. Thanks to the concept of social business, citizens don't have to leave all problems in the hands of the government (and then spend their lives criticizing the government for failing to solve them). Now citizens can have a completely new space in which to mobilize their creativity and talent for solving the problems of our time. Seeing the effectiveness of social business, governments may decide to create their own social businesses, partner with citizen-run social businesses, and incorporate the lessons from the social businesses to improve the effectiveness of their own programs.

Governments will have an important role to play in promoting social businesses. They will need to pass legislation to give legal recognition to social business and create regulatory bodies to ensure transparency, integrity, and honesty in this sector. They can also provide tax incentives for investing in social businesses as well as for social businesses themselves.

The wonderful promise of social business makes it all the more important that we redefine and broaden our present economic framework. We need a new way of thinking about economics that is not prone to creating a series of crises; instead it should be capable of ending the crises once and for all. Now is the time for bold and creative thinking—and we need to move fast, because the world is changing fast. The first piece of this new framework must be to accommodate social business as an integral part of the economic structure.

In just a few short years, social business has developed from a mere idea into a living, rapidly growing, reality. It is already bringing improvements into the lives of many people and is now on the verge of exploding into one of the world's most important social and economic trends. In the rest of this book, I'll explain more about the theory of social business, tell the stories of several social businesses that are already in action, and offer practical suggestions about how you can get involved in supporting this new movement.

CHAPTER 1

Why Social Business?

A social business is a new kind of business. It's quite distinct from either a traditional profit-maximizing business (which describes practically all private companies in the world today) or a not-for-profit organization (which relies on charitable or philanthropic donations). It's also quite distinct from some other frequently used terms, such as "social enterprise," "social entrepreneurship," or "socially responsible business," which generally describe varieties of profit-maximizing companies.

A social business is outside the profit-seeking world. Its goal is to solve a social problem by using business methods, including the creation and sale of products or services. Grameen Danone, for example, is working to solve the problem of malnutrition by selling affordable yogurt fortified with micronutrients. Grameen Veolia Water addresses the problem of arsenic-contaminated drinking water by selling pure water at a price the poor can afford. BASF Grameen will reduce mosquito-borne diseases by producing and marketing treated mosquito nets. There are many other examples—some already in operation, others in the making.

There are two kinds of social business. One is a non-loss, non-dividend company devoted to solving a social problem and owned by investors who reinvest all profits in expanding and improving the business. The examples mentioned above fit into this category. We call this a Type I social business.

The second kind is a profit-making company owned by poor people, either directly or through a trust that is dedicated to a predefined social cause. We call this a Type II social business. Since profits that flow to poor people are alleviating poverty, such a business is by definition helping to solve a social problem. Grameen Bank, which is owned by the poor people who are its depositors and customers, is an example of this kind of social business. And as I'll explain later in this book, the Otto Grameen textile factory, currently in the planning stages, will be a second example. It will be owned by Otto Grameen Trust, which will use the proceeds to benefit the people of the community where the factory is located.

Unlike a non-profit organization, a social business has investors and owners. However, in a Type I social business, the investors and owners don't earn a profit, a dividend, or any other form of financial benefit. The investors in a social business can take back their original investment amount over a period of time they define. It could be a very short period, such as one or two years, or a very long period, as much as fifty years or more. But any increase in the money going to investors beyond the original investment disqualifies the business from being a social business.

This even applies to an adjustment for inflation. In social business, a dollar is a dollar is a dollar. If you invest a thousand dollars in a social business, you'll get back a thousand dollars—not a penny more. We are strict about this because we want to make it very clear that the notion of personal financial benefit has no place in social business.

Because social business is a new idea, I've devoted a lot of time and energy to defining it precisely and figuring out ways to communicate its nature clearly and compellingly to the general public. An important ally in this effort has been Hans Reitz, director of the Grameen Creative Lab (GCL) in Wiesbaden, Germany. Reitz helped me formulate the Seven Principles of social business, which do a particularly good job of presenting the key characteristics of a Type I social business:

1. The business objective is to overcome poverty, or one or more problems (such as education, health, technology access, and environment) that threaten people and society—not to maximize profit.
2. The company will attain financial and economic sustainability.
3. Investors get back only their investment amount. No dividend is given beyond the return of the original investment.
4. When the investment amount is paid back, profit stays with the company for expansion and improvement.
5. The company will be environmentally conscious.
6. The workforce gets market wage with better-than-standard working conditions.
7. Do it with joy!!!

The last of the Seven Principles was Reitz's suggestion, and I must say, I like it. Caught up in the aggressive environment of conventional business, we forgot that business can have anything to do with joy. Social business is all about joy. Once you get involved with it you continue to discover the unlimited joy in doing it.

The Seven Principles are the core of social business. Keep them in mind as you read the rest of this book. You'll notice these principles at work when we describe specific social businesses that are already in operation as well as ideas for new social businesses that have yet to be launched. When companies and entrepreneurs meet with us to learn about the social business concept and explore ways to get involved in this movement, we share the Seven Principles with them. They serve as a touchstone and a constant reminder of the values that are at the heart of the social business idea.

What Social Business Is—and Is Not

Terms such as "social enterprise," "social entrepreneurship," and many others are frequently used in literature devoted to efforts to address problems such as poverty. Although these terms are used in varying ways by different writers, they are generally used to refer to subconcepts within either the profit-making world or the traditional world of non-profit organizations. Thus, they are *not* the same as what I call social business.

"Social entrepreneurship" relates to a person. It describes an initiative of social consequences created by an entrepreneur with a social vision. This initiative may be a non-economic initiative, a charity initiative, or a business initiative with or without personal profit. Some social entrepreneurs house their projects within traditional non-governmental organizations (NGOs), while others are involved in for-profit activities. In contrast with social entrepreneurship, social business is a very specific type of business—a non-loss, non-dividend company with a social objective. A social business may pursue goals similar to those sought by some social entrepreneurs, but the specific business structure of social business makes it distinctive and unique.

Some organizations that promote the concept of social entrepreneurship, such as the educational foundation Ashoka, list my work and that of Grameen Bank under this heading. I don't object, and Ashoka has done a good job of connecting people around the world with the Grameen story and the concept of microcredit. But it would be a mistake to lump together my work with that of all the other social entrepreneurs, or to assume that "social entrepreneurship" and "social business" are simply two names for the same thing.

Some people think that a social business is a kind of non-profit organization. This is not correct. Note some of the characteristics that distinguish a social business from the typical forms of non-profit organizations.

A foundation, for example, is a charitable organization created to disburse funds from one or more donors who seek to create social benefits through their giving. A foundation is not a social business: It is not financially self-sustaining, it normally does not generate any income through business activities, and it does not have an "owner" the way a social business does. (Under the laws of most countries, foundations and other non-profits are not owned but rather governed by boards of directors under guidelines established by the state.)

However, a foundation could *own* a social business. In fact, I think it could be an excellent use of foundation monies to establish social businesses within the organization's sphere of interest. When a foundation gives a grant to a traditional NGO, the money is spent to establish or support charitable programs, and hopefully it provides some benefits to the community. But in any case, the money is soon spent, and in most cases the NGO is soon applying for another grant to continue its work.

By contrast, if a foundation were to provide investment money with which to launch a social business, the business could create social benefits while generating the income to sustain itself. Over time it would repay the original investment, which means the foundation would get its money back and be able to use it for some other worthy purpose. Meanwhile, the social business would chug along, doing good in the world and, if it is well run, expanding and spreading its influence in ever-widening circles throughout the society.

As I'll explain later, there are legal and tax rules in some countries, including the United States, that make it complicated for a foundation to invest in a business. However, these complications can be overcome. I'd like to see foundations using some of their funds to establish social businesses in their areas of interest: health, education, and sustainable agriculture. I hope some of today's leading foundations are considering such possibilities.

In a similar way, a traditional NGO, which is a non-profit, charitable organization, could also own a social business. It would need to be separated from the NGO for legal, tax, and accounting purposes. But as long as the social business shares the same social objectives as the NGO, it seems to me that such an investment would be a wise and potentially powerful tool for pursuing the NGO's charitable goals.

NGOs do a lot of good work in the world. But the charitable model has some inherent weaknesses, which led me to create the concept of social business as an alternative.

Relying on charitable donations is not a sustainable way of running an organization. It forces NGO leaders to spend a lot of time, energy, and money on fund-raising efforts. Even when these are successful, most NGOs are perennially strapped for cash and unable to sustain, let alone expand, their most effective programs. By contrast, a social business is designed to be sustainable. This allows its owners to focus not on asking for donations, but on increasing the benefits they can deliver to the poor or to others in society. The power of the social business to endlessly recycle money gives it potentially far greater impact than even the best-run charity.

Furthermore, social business treats its beneficiaries with greater personal dignity and autonomy than charity. Even well-meaning, well-designed charity programs have the inevitable effect of taking away the initiative of those who receive the benefits. Poor people who become dependent on charity do not feel encouraged to stand on their own feet.

By contrast, people who pay a fair price for the goods and services they receive are taking a giant step toward self-reliance. Rather than passively accepting gifts, they are actively participating in the economic system, becoming players in their own right in our free-market economy. This is enormously empowering and leads much more directly to genuine, long-term solutions to such problems as poverty, inequality, and oppression.

Of course, not all charity should be replaced by social business. Sometimes simply helping people in desperate need is essential—for example, when a natural disaster such as the tsunami of 2004 or the terrible earthquake that devastated Haiti in 2010 destroys infrastructure, makes people homeless, and creates a huge need for food, medicine, and clothing. Families within a few days of starvation can't wait to launch businesses to support themselves—they need food, and they need it quickly. Charity is the only immediate response in such cases. But soon the emergency situation gives way to a phase when social business interventions can be very appropriate and immensely helpful. That's why we have created a Social Business Fund for Haiti to create a series of social businesses as longterm, sustainable solutions for the people of Haiti. Both charity and social businesses are needed, but we must understand how, and to what extent, each can contribute to reducing the misery of the people.

There are also some categories of people who unfortunately must rely on charity, because it is virtually impossible for them to support themselves. I'm thinking of people who suffer from extreme physical or mental disabilities, as well as the very old and the very young. As a society, we simply owe these people our help, and it would be cruel to insist that they support themselves. So there is room in our world for charity, just as there is room for social business.

However, I would point out that the potential sphere for social business, within which poor people can become self-sufficient, is greater than many people assume. I've mentioned the program by which Grameen Bank makes it possible for beggars to transform themselves into small business owners through tiny loans. This program has shown that even the poorest of the poor—people with no obvious skills or resources—can become self-supporting when the tools they need are made available.

Programs run by other organizations have worked similar "miracles" with other categories of human beings who are sometimes dismissed as hopeless: drug addicts, the physically disabled, the mentally ill. Let's not be quick to assume that people can be helped only by handouts. Instead, let's try to use our creativity to unlock the hidden potential that almost everyone has been given by God.

Another type of organization that might be confused with a social business is a cooperative.

A cooperative is owned by its members. It is run for profit to benefit the member-shareholders. When the cooperative movement was first created by socialists such as Robert Owen in the early nineteenth century, it had clear social objectives: to empower the poor, to encourage self-sufficiency, and to promote economic development. Today, some co-ops still create social benefits. For example, there are housing co-ops that make affordable homes available to working-class people, food co-ops that bring healthy nutrition within the reach of city dwellers, and banking co-ops that provide financial services to consumers who might otherwise be underserved.

However, some co-ops are run very much like ordinary profit-maximizing companies. They simply bring together collections of people or companies—farmers raising a particular crop, for example—and create a business structure within which they operate so as to increase their personal profits. There's nothing wrong with this. But it's not a social business.

Is it possible for a co-op to be a social business? Yes, if the members who own the co-op are poor people. In that case, any profits generated by the co-op would go to supporting the poor and helping them escape from poverty—which, by definition, is a socially beneficial activity. An example is the Self-Employed Women's Organisation (SEWA), a trade union that helps self-employed Indian women pursue the goals of "full employment": work security, income security, food security, health-care, child care, and shelter. Organized as a trade union for home textile workers in 1972, SEWA now has over 900,000 members throughout India. These members select their own leaders and effectively run the organization for the benefit of the rank-and-file.

Finally, let me mention one more term that I am sometimes asked about by people who are wondering what social business is. That term is "social marketing." It's a concept that surfaced among sociologists in the 1970s to describe efforts to change human behavior in a socially beneficial way by using tools and techniques drawn from business marketing. An example might be the antismoking campaigns that many governments and NGOs have developed using television commercials, statements from celebrities, and magazine advertisements to carry the message. Despite the similarity in name, social marketing of this kind has really nothing to do with my concept of social business.

Social Business and Corporate Social Responsibility

Corporate social responsibility (CSR) is another term that sometimes gets confused with social business. CSR often designates a charity fund set aside by a profit-maximizing company to do some good in the local community. For example, the CSR department of a company might donate money to a hospital or school, provide scholarships for a few poor children, or sponsor a cleanup day at the local beach or park. CSR programs are mostly used to build a company's image, to promote the idea that the company is a "good neighbor" or a "good citizen." There's nothing wrong with CSR, but it has no real relation to social business.

By contrast, a social business is directly devoted to changing the economic and social situation of the poor or to creating some other social improvement in the world. A profit-maximizing company that practices CSR may devote 95 percent of its resources to producing profits and 5 percent (or less) to making the world a better place. A social business devotes 100 percent of its resources to making the world a better place.

The CSR concept may also refer to certain rules of good citizenship that some enlightened business leaders try to live by. Not every business will be, or should be, a social business. But even traditional profit-maximizing businesses should follow some basic principles of responsibility.

The first responsibility principle that every business leader should follow is to make sure the business does not imperil anybody's life on this planet. I'd like to see every business manager take a personal vow to not make our world a riskier place than it would be without the business in it. This means operating the business in a safe manner—for example, following procedures to avoid the risk of injuries to workers.

It means making products and services that are safe to use. And it means taking steps to avoid polluting the environment or contributing to global warming. It seems to me that a company that considers itself to be devoted to the principles of CSR should practice at least these minimal steps.

The second responsibility principle goes a bit further. It states that the business will contribute to making the planet safer than it would have been without the business. Under this principle, it's not enough merely to refrain from polluting—it's also necessary to help clean up the atmosphere, the seas, and the ground we walk on, leaving them in better shape than we found them. It's not enough simply to produce goods that don't harm the customers—it's also necessary to create products that make life easier, safer, and more healthful for those who use them.

And the third responsibility principle is that the business should be conducted within the framework of social and political responsibilities established by the state and global authorities. Of course, this means obeying laws and regulations regarding safety, environmental responsibility, financial integrity, and so on. But it also means actively contributing to business efforts to support the well-being of society on the local, national, and global levels. Companies that believe in CSR should strive to be good corporate citizens, helping to make the world a better place through their policies, procedures, and practices.

Based on principles like these, we can design businesses where there is no conflict between social and economic objectives. "Social" means in this context that the business serves to benefit a broad group of people rather than being focused purely on the shareholders' monetary gain. There is no reason why we cannot design such businesses—this kind of social undertaking makes perfect economic sense. But again, it is not the same as a social business as I've defined it.

As an example, consider the company The Sun Shines for All. This for-profit business, founded by the social entrepreneur Fabio Rosa, is dedicated to providing solar electricity to rural Brazilians. Rosa studied villagers in the southernmost state of Brazil, Rio Grande do Sul, where few people are connected to the regional power grid. He found that almost 70 percent of the families spent at least $11 per month on energy sources such as kerosene, candles, batteries, and liquid petroleum gas. This is the same amount of money they could instead be spending to rent a basic home solar electric system, including wiring, lights, and outlets for appliances. Such a system would be environmentally sustainable, more healthful, and more versatile.

Rosa's company is now installing this kind of solar energy system in villages throughout southern Brazil. He hopes to eventually reach over three-quarters of a million homes that currently have no electricity. Clearly this is a social benefit to the poor people of Brazil. But The Sun Shines for All is not a social business. The business plan calls for an internal rate of return between 29 and 30 percent—a figure Rosa calculates is necessary to attract profit-seeking foreign investors.

Profit-seeking companies with a strong CSR commitment try to make their pursuit of profit consistent with social considerations. However, their commitment to making a profit inevitably limits their contributions to social causes. Under the present economic framework that defines the profit-maximizing company, they have to design the company to pursue profit first and then add the social features—provided the social features don't interfere with maximizing profit.

It's a tricky balancing act. For example, what will happen if one day the economic conditions in Brazil force Rosa to choose between a high rate of profit for his outside investors and affordable rental fees for his rural electricity customers? Because Rosa's company is organized as a traditional for-profit business, it's possible that service to the community would have to suffer to keep investors satisfied. This is a choice a social business doesn't have to make.

By contrast, a social business is designed exclusively to deliver social benefits. There is no thought of creating profit for any investor. As a result, it becomes very powerful, and its attention to the social cause is totally undivided.

Is social business better than normal business? It depends on what you consider better or worse. If you want to make money, then a profit-maximizing company is of course better. If you want to solve people's problems, social business is the way forward. Profit-making companies cannot do this job—or not nearly as well.

Profit and Social Business

Some people ask, why exclude the idea of *combining* the power of the profit principle with the goal of social benefit—or "doing well by doing good," as it is sometimes phrased? If the only aim is to eradicate poverty, for instance, should we not be pragmatic about how to get there? This might also include being pragmatic about the issue of profit. Some people might argue that a profit-making organization can more successfully fight poverty. The prospect of making a profit might allow them to attract more capital, to expand their model faster, and hence to touch more lives, more quickly. This is the notion of the "double bottom line" or "triple bottom line" that some well-intentioned businesspeople talk about.

I am not opposed to making profit. Even social businesses are allowed to earn a profit, with the condition that the profit stays with the company and is used to expand the social benefits the company provides. (I often use the word "surplus" to make a clearer distinction between this kind of profit and the profits earned by conventional businesses, which go to benefit the owners.) Profit in itself is not a bad thing.

However, social business is a new category of business. It does not stipulate the end of the familiar profit-maximizing business model. Rather, it widens the market by giving a new option to consumers, employees, and entrepreneurs. It brings a new dimension to the business world and a new feeling of social awareness among business people.

To be perfectly clear: I am not asking businesspeople to give up any of their businesses. Nor am I asking them to convert their businesses into social businesses. All I am saying is this: If you are worrying about a social problem, you can make a significant contribution to resolving the problem through the mechanism of social business. It is up to you to decide whether you want to do such a thing. Nobody will raise an accusing finger at you if you choose the path of conventional business instead. But you may feel happy if you follow the social business path. I for one can testify that this is very possible!

So I have no intention of trying to coerce anyone into starting or joining a social business. But I do want to explicitly define social business as excluding the pursuit of profit or the payment of dividends to owners. There are three main reasons why this is important.

First, there is the moral argument. I believe it's immoral to make a profit—and especially to pursue the usual business goal of maximum profit—from the poor. In effect, this is benefiting from the suffering of our fellow human beings. It seems to me that common human decency forbids such a thing.

This is not merely a theoretical argument. The issue is a very real one within the microcredit community. Over the past twenty years, as the power of the Grameen Bank model of microcredit has become widely recognized, organizations around the world have begun offering small loans to poor people.

Many of these organizations follow closely the methods that Grameen Bank pioneered—including charging the lowest possible interest rates on loans and giving borrowers the opportunity to become owners of the bank. (At Grameen Bank, our highest interest rate is 20 percent, and many types of loans, including student loans and home mortgages, are assessed at significantly lower rates.)

However, some for-profit companies in the microcredit world have become very financially successful by charging much higher interest rates, sometimes in excess of 80 percent or even 100 percent per year. They defend these rates by saying that lending to the poor is very expensive. It's true that it costs more to manage small loans to poor people than conventional loans. But interest rates should not go too far beyond the sum of the cost of funds and the delivery cost.

I have spoken out against these excessive charges, which violate the spirit in which microcredit was originally created—the spirit of serving the poor. Replacing the traditional exploitative village money-lender with a new form of exploitation was not what I had in mind when I founded Grameen Bank.

When businesspeople ask me about the profits to be made in serving the poorest people in the world, I sometimes reply, "I have no quarrel with the pursuit of profit. But first let's give the poor people the help they need to escape from poverty. Once they have become middle class, then I urge you to sell them all the goods and services you can—and make a handsome profit doing so! But wait until they are no longer poor before you exploit them. That is the only right thing to do."

My second argument for defining social business as strictly avoiding the pursuit of profit is a pragmatic one. In times of stress, profit will always trump the other "bottom lines."

When you mix profit and social benefit, and say that your company will pursue *both* goals, you are making life complicated for the CEO. His thinking process gets clouded. He does not see clearly. In a particular situation where profit and social benefit need to be balanced, which way should the scales be tipped? What if it is possible to increase profit greatly by cutting social benefits just a little—is that all right? How should one judge? What about in times of economic stress, like a recession—is it all right to eliminate social benefits altogether in hopes of helping the company to survive? Why or why not? The idea of a "mixed" company offers no clear guidance on questions like these.

In practice, profit tends to win out in struggles of this kind. Most often the CEO will lean—perhaps unconsciously—in favor of profit, and exaggerate the social benefits being created. And if the CEO is a little unclear about the *real* priority, we can imagine that the middle managers and line employees will be even more uncertain. Over time, the social goals will gradually fade in importance, while the need to make money becomes more and more deeply ingrained in the company's culture.

Here is a small example. In the United States, many poor people rely on local food banks to stave off hunger. These food banks, in turn, rely on donations from individuals as well as companies to keep their shelves stocked with foods that can be donated to hungry families.

In recent years, many food banks have been supported by grocery stores that donate outdated, dented, or mislabeled packages of food that they can't sell. Hungry people are happy to receive these "unsellable" items, and the grocers get the benefit of being good community members. It's a fine example of how corporate social responsibility is supposed to work.

In the fall of 2009, however, many food banks in the United States reported a shortfall in donations. One reason is that a new business has emerged in which middlemen buy "unsellable" merchandise from grocers for 30 or 40 cents on the dollar. These middlemen, in turn, sell the goods to low-price stores, which sell them to consumers at a steep discount from the usual price. It's a new source of profits to the grocers—but it means that the once-unsellable food is no longer available to be donated to the food banks.

I can't really blame the grocers for taking advantage of this new avenue of business. Their job is to maximize profit in any way they can. But this example illustrates the danger in leaving the needs of the poor to be served through the generosity of profit-maximizing companies. When profit and human needs conflict, profit generally wins out—which means that people lose.

Social business gives a clear, unambiguous mandate to management. There is no balancing act involved. Every decision the company makes can be measured against a single yardstick: What will enable us to provide the greatest possible benefit to society? This doesn't mean that the decisions are always easy—creative problem-solving is just as difficult in social business as in profit-maximizing business. But at least the manager isn't forced to juggle two sets of mutually contradictory objectives.

Third is the systemic argument. It is necessary to create social business as a clearly defined alternative, separate from the worlds of business and charity, in order to change mindsets, reshape economic structures, and encourage new forms of thinking.

For many people, the biggest challenge seems to be getting over the hurdle of the no-profit rule itself. "Can't we take a *small* profit?" I am sometimes asked. It seems as though the idea of profit is like a familiar crutch that businesspeople are afraid to throw away.

Trust me, it can be done! If you can agree to take a "small" profit (however that is defined), you can also persuade yourself to take zero profit. Once you get there, you find yourself in a new world, seeing and doing things in a new way.

Consider this analogy: Suppose you are trying to quit smoking. Would it be helpful or the opposite to allow yourself to take "just one small puff"? The answer is simple—"a little bit" of backsliding destroys the whole attitude. In the holy month of Ramadan, Muslims are not allowed to eat or drink until after sunset. Why not take a small snack, or even a sip of water, during the day? It would destroy the strength of the mental commitment. In the same way, making a complete break from the for-profit attitude creates a huge and important difference for the businessperson who really wants to commit himself or herself to social change.

Social business is about totally delinking from the old framework of business—not accommodating new objectives within the existing framework. Until you make this total delinking from personal financial gain, you'll never discover the power of real social business.

Let's be very honest: The profit motive is extremely powerful. Once it gets its nose under the edge of the tent, it soon takes over the entire dwelling space.

This is the problem with traditional capitalism, which is such a creative and effective force for good in so many ways. Capitalism has created poverty by focusing exclusively on profit. It built a fairy tale of prosperity for all—a dream that was doomed never to come true. That's why many European countries decided to empower their governments to take care of social needs, such as poverty, unemployment, education, and healthcare. They were smart enough to figure out the inability of traditional capitalism to solve these problems.

In the developing world, however, government lacks the managerial ability and material resources to create the kind of welfare state Europeans enjoy. In some other countries, such as the United States, cultural and political norms prevent government from addressing social problems. For these and other reasons, a new mechanism is needed. Social business can be that mechanism—provided it is kept completely free from the complication of profit-seeking. Being in social business is like being in a no-smoking zone—even a tiny little puff spoils the whole concept.

The Origin of the Social Business Idea

The origin of the idea of social business was really quite simple: Whenever I wanted to deal with a social or economic problem, I tried to solve the problem by creating a business around it. Over time I became convinced that it is an excellent way to address social and economic problems, but one that is missing in the framework of economic theory. I strongly feel that it should be included. This missing piece in the theoretical framework is what I call social business.

It all started because my work with Grameen Bank brought me into contact with lots of poor people, many of whom had problems that went beyond a simple lack of credit. For example, consider the Sixteen Decisions—the set of commitments that we ask each Grameen Bank borrower to make in order to strengthen herself, her family, and her potential for growth. The Sixteen Decisions were developed in the early years of Grameen Bank and finalized in 1984. Since then, they have remained an integral part of Grameen Bank's business approach.

What's important to notice is that the Sixteen Decisions are not about banking. For example, Decision Four states, "We shall grow vegetables all the year round. We shall eat plenty of them and sell the surplus." This decision became part of the Grameen program because we noticed that many of the families we served suffered from conditions such as night blindness due to vitamin A deficiency. This was a problem that was within their power to solve—so why not solve it?

Similarly, Decision Nine says, "We shall build and use pit latrines." Most Grameen Bank borrowers live in communities without modern sanitary systems. A pit latrine is a simple, practical way of drastically reducing the incidence of diseases spread by contact with human waste. All in all, nine of the sixteen decisions are related to health: safe housing, cleanliness, safe drinking water, family planning, and so on.

This is how the Grameen organizations got involved in social issues beyond simply providing financial services—and how we began to think about creating programs to improve every element in the lives of poor families.

Around each problem we identified, we created separate programs. And then, over time, we created company after company, each one dedicated to addressing a different social problem we'd observed through our interactions with the poor people of Bangladesh.

A complete description of all the Grameen companies would run for many pages. Here I'll offer just a brief explanation of some of the most important examples. (If you are curious, you can learn more about the Grameen family of companies in *Creating a World Without Poverty.*)

- *Grameen Telecom* and *Grameen Phone* have made modern telecommunications available to people throughout Bangladesh, with enormous economic and social benefits. Grameen Phone, a mobile phone company, was launched in 1996 and quickly expanded its network coverage to cover the whole country. By the middle of 2009, Grameen Phone had become the largest tax-paying company in Bangladesh, with over 25 million subscribers. Grameen Bank would provide a loan to a Grameen borrower to buy a cell phone and become the telephone lady of the village by selling telephone service, one call at a time, to those without phones of their own. More than 400,000 telephone ladies were created through this program.

- *Grameen Shakti (Grameen Energy, 1995)* has become the fastest growing solar home system company in the world. It sells 14,000 solar home systems per month to the villagers in Bangladesh. By the end of 2010 it will have half a million solar home systems in operation in these villages. It will also have half a million improved cooking stoves and 50,000 bio-gas plants in operation.

- *Grameen Kalyan (Grameen Wellbeing, 1997)* exists to provide good-quality, affordable healthcare for Grameen Bank borrowers and other villagers. It operates fifty-four health clinics and offers a health insurance program providing basic healthcare to families for the equivalent of around $2 per year per family. We are now in the process of building up a nationwide healthcare system through a series of social businesses specializing in providing healthcare.

- *Grameen Fisheries and Livestock Foundation* was launched in 1986 to administer nearly 1,000 fish ponds in northern and western Bangladesh that had become moribund under poor management by a government agency. By the end of 2009, we had organized over 3,000 poor people into groups who produce 2,000 tons of fish per year, work to maintain the ponds, and receive nearly half of the produce in exchange for a share of the gross income. In 2002, a livestock program was added, providing training, vaccination, veterinary care, and other support services to help poor women become dairy farmers and assist others in improving and expanding existing dairy operations.

- *Grameen Shikkha (Grameen Education)* was created in 1997 to provide education to the children of our borrowers, including preschool classes held at Grameen Bank centers. In 2003, it was expanded to include a Scholarship Management Program, which created an endowment fund for generating scholarships for poor students. By 2009, it had accumulated enough in the endowment fund to provide scholarships to 2,500 poor students. It continues to expand the endowment to finance more and more scholarships each year.

- *Grameen Uddog (1993)* and *Grameen Shamogree (1996)* are textile companies that we created to revive and modernize the traditional Bangladeshi handloom industry of manufacturing beautiful cotton fabrics and garments. Grameen Uddog (Grameen Enterprise) helped local weavers bring to the international markets a new, uniform line of fabrics under the brand name of Grameen Check. Grameen Shamogree (Grameen Products) focuses on local sales of Grameen Check garments.

Each of these Grameen businesses was created with its own business plan, organizational form, mission statement, and financial structure. Each was refined, improved, and modified on the basis of growing experience as to what worked and what didn't. And each new business benefited from the insights generated by the experiences with the ones that came before.

Eventually I looked back at what we had accomplished and realized that the Grameen family of businesses was different from traditional businesses. Conventional companies exist to make money; these exist to solve social problems while using business techniques and models. In time, I gave this new form of business a precise definition and a name: social business. Most of the businesses I had already created did not fit the definition exactly, so I started creating new businesses to fit the definition I'd developed. I elaborated my ideas about it in *Creating a World Without Poverty.* Many people responded enthusiastically, and that is how social business came to be a rapidly growing social and economic movement.

I often speak about the potential of social business when discussing my dream of a world in which poverty no longer exists. Perhaps because of this ambitious context, I am often asked, "How long will it take for this new movement to make an impact on global society?"

I honestly don't know how long it will take for humankind to wipe out the scourge of poverty (although I firmly believe it can happen much sooner than most people assume—say within the period of 2030 to 2050). But for those who are considering becoming involved in social business, *you don't have to wait.* You can see the impact right away—not on the whole of society, but on a portion of it.

I urge anyone who has an idea for a social business to start work on it as soon as possible. Even if it improves life for only five people— by lifting them out of poverty, providing them with a home, or bringing them affordable healthcare—it is worth undertaking. It's not necessary to wait to see the impact on millions of people. "Millions" is a big number. But if your work has a positive impact on five or ten people, you have invented a seed. Now you can plant it a million times.

Remember, that's how Grameen Bank got started—with loans totaling $27. It never crossed my mind to ask, "Will this solve the problems of 50 million poor people in Bangladesh?" I was simply asking myself, "Can I do something to help the villagers of Jobra?" When I solved the problem of a few people, I felt encouraged. I realized that all I had to do was to keep on repeating it. As a result, microcredit became a global phenomenon. If you know how to lend money to five people, you have learned how to do it for five thousand people—or five hundred million.

Social Business and Government

Sometimes people ask me whether social business is somehow akin to socialism or communism. Having grown accustomed to many years of two-way rivalry between capitalism on one side and communism on the other, they may assume that anyone who notices flaws in the theory and practice of capitalism must somehow be allied with the socialists. In socialism and communism, the state (meaning the government) controls the economy. Major portions of the economy—or, in some systems, the whole economy—are kept under the command of government bureaucrats or politicians. Economic decisions are made based on political considerations. There is virtually no competition among business enterprises. In time, efficiency and innovation tend to disappear.

Social business offers an *option* to investors. It is not forced on anybody. It operates in an open economy with free choice. All players in the marketplace are welcome to create their own social businesses— businesses, governments, individuals, foundations, or any other social or economic entity. Nobody is excluded. Social business helps citizens to undertake activities which traditionally were considered the responsibilities of the government. As a result, government's burden is lightened, its efforts complemented by those of civil society. Governments can collaborate with social businesses run by civil society and businesses, since social businesses are not run by profit-takers, and at the same time governments can create their own social businesses.

The existence of social business means that businesses, civil society, and individual people now have access to a business format that they can use to tackle major social problems. In a society where social business is a vibrant economic force, people will no longer have to wait for the government to address such issues as poverty, hunger, homelessness, and diseases because they themselves can find ways to address them by forming their own enterprises, first on a small scale and eventually on a large scale.

Furthermore, social business enhances competition and freedom of choice by giving people more choices of goods and services. When the social business sector flourishes alongside traditional profit-maximizing companies, consumers will have more sources to choose from. At the same time, workers and managers will have more career options. Social business emphasizes bottom-up growth and experimentation by thousands or millions of individuals who are free to create any kind of organization they want to pursue their choice of personal and social goals.

Social business recognizes that the responsibility for solving a society's problems is shared between the government and the citizens. What's more, it recognizes the abilities individuals have that government does not. Smart, talented, creative individuals can produce innovations that government is rarely capable of developing. And they do this without imposing any economic burden on anybody. Government uses taxpayer money in its attempts to solve social problems, and therefore it is limited by its resource base. Social business, by contrast, can be expanded indefinitely by raising investment money from every imaginable source.

In theory, government should represent all the people and therefore should bear the chief responsibility for addressing social problems that create human suffering. In some fortunate countries, this happens to a greater or lesser extent. But in practice, governments often become captive to special interests, self-serving political parties, and corrupt individuals. Hence the need for social business. If governments had already solved the world's most pressing problems, we would not need social business. But throughout the world, in poor countries and rich countries alike, social problems are plaguing humankind—welfare dependency, unemployment, crime, lack of housing and healthcare, environmental degradation, obesity, chronic disease . . . the list goes on and on.

Of course, those of us who advocate social business don't have blueprints for solving all these problems, nor do we claim to. But we do know that government efforts have fallen short and that a new approach is necessary. In many cases, social business offers a promising alternative to failed government programs.

Think about the government programs in your own community or country that have led to disappointing results. They might include public schools, hospital systems, transit companies, water and sanitation services, energy utilities, airports and seaports, highway networks, and other similar institutions. Until now, the only alternative to government control has been the concept of "privatization"—which all too often simply means handing over public property to well-connected individuals who then exploit their new holdings for private gain.

Instead, why not experiment with making some of these government operations into social businesses, with the explicit mission of serving the needs of the people? This could be a way of combining the creativity and energy of business with the avowed social purpose of government, producing shared benefits that neither sector has produced before.

Social Business as a New Form of Capitalism

To this point, I've been emphasizing the differences between social business and traditional profit-maximizing business. But the similarities are just as important.

Look at a couple of the first social businesses we've created in Bangladesh. Grameen Danone is a yogurt company that produces, markets, and distributes its products much the same as any for-profit yogurt company. Grameen Veolia Water treats surface water for contaminants and then pipes it to where it is needed, much like the water systems that Veolia Water and other companies operate around the world. In these ways, these two social businesses are very much like other companies.

Of course, these companies have some unique qualities as well. The yogurt produced by Grameen Danone is fortified for nutritional purposes, which creates a challenge: how to mask the taste of the vitamins and minerals so that youngsters will like and eat the product. In this case, meeting the social need requires a product formulation solution—using business creativity to solve a health-related challenge.

Grameen Veolia Water is wrestling with the problem of convincing rural villagers to spend some of their sparse family income on drinking water, a product they are accustomed to getting for free. Again, the healthcare problem requires a smart business solution—in this case, one that is marketing oriented.

I'll provide more details about the challenges these two companies face later in this book. But already you can see that there is a pattern here. The social businesses operate within the same capitalist system as conventional businesses. Like profit-maximizing companies, they must find ways to sell their products that will cover all their costs and perhaps generate enough money to fund expansion. They must respond effectively to market challenges, price their offerings so that the target audience of poor people can afford them, and, when possible, take advantage of opportunities to generate additional income through sales at higher prices to more affluent customers. Like other types of businesses, a social business can grow or shrink, and it can expect to face many of the same kinds of problems: financing, talent recruitment, management, expansion, and so on.

In other words, social businesses are subject to many of the same market signals, stresses, and challenges as profit-making businesses. However, a social business has one advantage. It is less exposed to downside risk in times when markets fluctuate, because the future of the business is not tied to its stock price. Since social business investors are not seeking personal gain, they will be more patient in waiting for results and less likely to abandon their ownership stake because of a few days or weeks of disappointing performance. This should make it easier for social businesses to develop sound long-term plans for achieving their objectives.

Above all, social business represents a new way for human beings to express their entrepreneurial spirit.

An entrepreneur is a risk-taker, a person driven by the burning desire to put his business idea into action. He is ready to tackle difficulties, to experiment boldly, to work long hours, and to experience personal setbacks and disappointments without becoming discouraged. He is not satisfied until his project is implemented successfully, producing the desired results—either financial reward (in the case of a profit-maximizing business) or social improvement (in the case of a social business).

My sense is that the special brand of entrepreneurship demanded by social business is quite similar to that required by a for-profit company. I'm sure it would be helpful to have experience from the world of conventional business, provided one knows how to adapt this experience for social business purposes. A business education, such as an MBA degree, may be useful if the person learns how to apply the learning to social business success. If he does not, the traditional business training may become an obstacle. The most appropriate thing would be to earn a "Social MBA" degree, a new form of education that I hope will soon be offered. More important are the personal qualities that mark the true entrepreneur. To be successful in social business, you need good practical business sense, a willingness to work hard, team-building capacity, the ability to connect with people whose collaboration you need, the ability to judge the results of your actions, and the honesty to admit when you've made a mistake and need to start over.

It is obvious that if you bring extensive background or knowledge from traditional business, you'll need to be willing to reorient yourself. In the world of social business, all your calculations will have a different purpose. You'll still be eager to find ways of reducing costs—but not by cutting the pay or benefits you offer to the poor people who may make up your workforce. You'll still look for smart ways to segment your customer base—but you won't want to use your market power to extract value from one set of people to enrich another. You'll still be trying to make your product or service as affordable as possible—but not if it means cutting corners on quality and thereby reducing the benefits you deliver to your customers. All of the business savvy you've developed in conventional business will be very useful, but the goals and values you'll pursue will be different.

Entrepreneurship is an integral part of human nature. Social business offers a new and exciting way of expressing it—not only for those people who may not feel comfortable with the restricted, one-track pursuit of profit that marks conventional business, but also for those who are quite comfortable in the profit-making world. Nobody is excluded from social business. Everybody is welcome to find the roles that work best for them—as investors, executives, creative advisers, promoters, marketers, managers, suppliers, producers, service agents, or whatever. The important thing is to get involved and to find your own way of making a positive difference in the world.

What Social Business Offers You

At this point, you may be starting to wonder, "What does the social business concept mean for me personally?" I hope you are—because one purpose of this book is to help people see that social business can be a wonderful way of enriching our own life experiences.

The motivation for starting or joining a social business is simple. It begins with the idealism and hope that are deeply ingrained in all human beings.

If you have ever found yourself thinking, "I don't like the way things are around me; it's painful to live in a world where hunger, poverty, disease, illiteracy, and unemployment afflict so many people; I want to see these terrible things disappear," then social business may be part of your life's calling.

Social business also provides an outlet for the creativity that millions of people harbor within themselves. "Creativity" doesn't have to mean something grand. It can be as simple as noticing a local problem and thinking, "I wonder whether anyone has ever tried to solve the problem by doing *this*"—and then trying it. A small local solution can become the seed of a global solution.

But even creativity on this modest scale is not a prerequisite. If you cannot develop a seed, you can pick up an existing seed and plant it in a new location. Social business offers many options. I like that.

Social business also offers an opportunity for individual renewal. Millions of people in every walk of life dream about change, but somehow never manage to experience it. Many of us feel trapped in "secure" lives that never leave the treadmill of routine work and unthinking consumption. At the same time, we wish we could escape into a different way of life where we can leave our signatures on this planet and discover the endless talents buried within us. Social business is a new way of framing our existence that offers the opportunity to redesign our lives even as we improve the planet we inhabit.

Social business, I've found, is a great learning process. Take the plunge and you quickly discover you are acting and thinking in ways you never did before. New challenges arise that force you to exercise intellectual and emotional muscles that have long gone unused. Past experiences that you'd almost forgotten suddenly become relevant and useful. You are exploring a new world that was totally unknown to you. Thanks to the "social business glasses" you now wear, you see things you never saw before. Slowly you move toward becoming a multidimensional person, rather than a robotic being driven solely by profit.

Social business is exciting and fun. For many people, the chief obstacle to making the commitment to social business is attitudinal. It's easy to lapse back into apathy, pessimism, and despair.

Many people argue that there is no point in trying to change the world, whether through social business or any other means—that the world has always been the same, and that there is no way to change human nature.

This is simply false. Today's world is not the same as the world in which our ancestors lived. We don't have plagues. We don't have slavery. We don't have monarchy. We don't have apartheid. We have women voting, free markets flourishing in once-closed societies, people around the world demanding human rights—even a black president in the United States. Change *does* happen, and that change is shaped by us.

As for human nature, my belief is that it is fundamentally good. That is why religion, good governance, social values, arts, culture, and charity have flourished throughout history, even in the face of tyranny and selfishness. The sprouts of justice and mercy are always struggling to grow through the cracks. If we nurture and nourish them, we can make this planet into the garden all humans dream of inhabiting.

An Idea Whose Time Has Come

We live in exciting times—an era when the world is ripe for the kind of amazing, positive change that social business can create.

I've mentioned the global economic crisis that began in 2008, exposing the weaknesses in traditional capitalist theory. But a crisis is also an opportunity for reform. Today's crisis gives us an opportunity to reshape economic theory so it reflects the multifaceted reality of human nature.

Furthermore, the current crisis—or, more accurately, the intertwined economic, environmental, agricultural, energy, health, and social crises—provides an opportunity for bold experimentation with new solutions. Social business has a better chance of changing the world than some past ideas because the concept is so powerful yet so flexible and accommodating. Social business involves no compulsion on anybody. It widens the scope of free choice rather than narrowing it down. It fits neatly into the capitalist system, offering the hope of bringing millions of new customers into the marketplace. Rather than threatening the existing structure of business, it proposes a way to revitalize it.

What's more, social business helps the governments share their burden of responsibilities for social change with the civil society. It also helps governments avoid creating or widening any political divides by undertaking a particular social action for the whole nation. Now governments can encourage social businesses to flourish in as many directions as they want, so that people can figure out which action is preferable to them without creating political crises. It is up to individuals to conceive, design, and create social businesses. Then the free market will decide which social businesses succeed and which ones fail. A social business concept can be developed on a trial-and-error basis and implemented slowly or quickly. It can be dormant for a while but remain alive, waiting for the right moment to shower its benefits on society. Like life itself, social business is capable of endless change, development, and growth.

Like any other idea, that of social business is subject to being misused and perverted. A few powerful people will look for ways to distort the concept and twist it for their own benefit—just as some misguided people have applied the term "microcredit" to describe companies that are really just loan sharks in disguise. Well-intentioned people will need to be on guard against those who would abuse the good name of social business.

But that's true for any basic concept. The ultimate fate of social business will depend on whether it has touched any special chord in people's hearts. If social business becomes part of people's dream of a better world, then nobody can stop it. It will flourish, even under adverse circumstances.

The time will come when social business is not only an accepted part of the capitalist system but is especially prized for its creative and idealistic approach to the world. Parents who today encourage their children to earn pocket money by delivering newspapers or setting up a lemonade stand on a summer day will urge them to start small social businesses aimed at solving neighborhood problems—planting trees, caring for homeless animals, running errands for elderly neighbors. Reality TV shows that today focus on opportunities in show business will challenge contestants to develop innovative new social business ideas, with a top prize of generous funding for the best idea so that it can quickly spread around the country and the world.

Personally, I see no upper limit to the role of social business in the global economy. In the years to come, social business may become a significant proportion of the business world as a whole. Theoretically, a whole economy could be made up of social businesses. If that happens, it will be as a result of people's free choices, not because of coercion. The ultimate role of social business will depend on what all the people want. Is there an optimal ratio between the two kinds of businesses—for individuals, for society, for the world? And how far can social business take us down the path toward a more perfect world, where every human being has the opportunity to live a life of dignity, freedom, and peace?

During the lifetimes of our children and our grandchildren, humankind will engage in an exciting experiment that will reveal the answers to questions like these. As the rest of this book will show, the experiment is already under way.

CHAPTER 2

Growing Pains

Lessons in Adaptation and
Change from the Story of Grameen Danone

In my last book, *Creating a World Without Poverty*, I told the story of Grameen Danone, the world's first consciously designed social business. At the time I completed that book, in early 2007, the Grameen Danone yogurt factory in Bogra, Bangladesh, was just going on line. The first cups of Shokti Doi yogurt, fortified with nutrients badly needed by the children of Bangladesh, were being produced, and the Grameen ladies who had been recruited to serve as local salespeople were beginning to take it to their friends and neighbors.

We were very excited about this pioneering effort to demonstrate that a social business could be self-sustaining while also creating important benefits to its customers, suppliers, and other community members. Grameen Danone's plan was to use the success of the first yogurt factory as a springboard to expanding the concept throughout the country. The company hoped to soon begin building a network of up to fifty small factories that could provide nutritious Shokti Doi to children all over Bangladesh.

As so often happens in life, it has not turned out to be so easy.

Over the past three years, Grameen Danone gained valuable experience in this business. There was a steady growth in sales for a full year after the launch of the business—then a collapse due to economic factors no one had predicted. The company had to reinvent its sales and distribution system, redesign its business model, modify the formula for the product, reach out to new groups of customers, and introduce new products for various segments of consumers.

In 2010, we are back on a steep growth curve, one we hope will prove to be long-lasting. In February, we surpassed the magic production figure of 100 tons per month, which is very close to the level we need to cover all operational costs and generate a surplus to cover fixed costs. We plan to expand the Bogra plant's capacity to 200 tons per month by adding a few facilities, and we are proceeding full speed to start production in our second plant near Dhaka in November of 2010. This is promising to be an exciting year for Grameen Danone.

But one thing is certain—along the way, we've all learned a lot about the challenges in building a sustainable social business. Some are problems that any company is likely to experience. Others are peculiar to the social business model. And all have taught us lessons we think will be valuable to us in the future, as well as to others who are interested in creating social businesses. That's why I think the story of Grameen Danone is one worth sharing.

Birth of a Social Business

Grameen Danone was born in a conversation between me and Franck Riboud, the chairman and CEO of Groupe Danone. During a lunch in Paris I proposed to Riboud, "Why don't we create a Grameen Danone in Bangladesh as a social business?" He liked the sound of the idea. But he wanted to know, "What is social business?" After I explained the concept—a business that sustains itself but whose purpose is to create social benefits rather than to generate a profit—Riboud was intrigued. Better still, he was ready to sign on.

"Let's do it," he said. And from that simple agreement, Grameen Danone was born.

Talented managers from our two organizations spent the next year or more developing the idea for our social business. Danone's expertise meant that nutrition would be a natural focus for the business. This was certainly an area of great need among the poor people of Bangladesh. Half of all the children in my country suffer from malnutrition, especially in rural areas. Diarrhea, often a byproduct of malnutrition, is much more than the nuisance it is in Western countries—it is often fatal.

Among the most common nutritional deficiencies are iron (suffered by 49 percent of young children); vitamins A, B2, and C; calcium; iodine; and zinc. Lack of these nutrients causes a range of problems, from immune system malfunctions to poor eyesight. And, of course, in the long run, widespread malnutrition reduces the prospects for economic development, since children who are ill-fed have difficulty growing up to be well-educated, energetic, productive adults.

After much discussion, we decided that the best way to start our joint venture would be with a yogurt business. Yogurt is not only a product for which Danone is famous the world over. It's also a traditional snack in Bangladesh, very popular among all people, including children. What's more, yogurt is a natural dairy product filled with calcium and protein, both essential nutrients that many young Bangladeshis lack.

We realized that if we could create a yogurt brand that was fortified with vitamins and other nutrients, appealing to children, and affordable for the poor, we could provide an important benefit to families in Bangladesh. We could reduce rates of illness, improve children's energy level, and increase their rates of participation in school and other worthwhile activities.

Of course, this was just the outline of our idea. Developing the complete business plan turned out to be quite complex. Danone's executive vice president for Asia Pacific operations, Emmanuel Faber, now co-CEO of Groupe Danone, brought a team of nutritionists, business planners, production specialists, and other experts to meet and work with us in Bangladesh throughout 2006. From Grameen Kalyan, our social business focused on healthcare, my good friend Imamus Sultan, who intimately knew the needs of the poor people of Bangladesh and had worked closely with me on many Grameen projects, was selected to work closely with Faber.

A handful of decisions were especially crucial. One was the decision to build a *small* yogurt factory rather than a large facility like a global company like Danone typically constructs. This would have several benefits. It would minimize the investment risk to Danone by reducing the up-front costs; it would limit the distribution area to a small one, eliminating the need for costly refrigerated trucks and warehouses; and it would simplify the problem of staffing the plant, since a small factory would require only a few workers rather than scores or hundreds.

Most important, a small factory would become part of the local community and economy. It could draw its supply of raw materials, especially milk, from local suppliers, and local consumers would be its chief customers. I hoped that people around the Grameen Danone plant would come to think of it as "*our* factory" and would support the business accordingly.

Working cooperatively, the Grameen and Danone teams selected a location near the city of Bogra, about 140 miles northwest of Dhaka, the capital of Bangladesh, to build the first plant. Danone sent Guy Gavelle, industrial director of the company's Asia Pacific operations, to design the plant and oversee its construction. Gavelle had built Danone facilities around the world, from China to Brazil, but he had never built a *tiny* factory before. Nevertheless, he was up for the challenge, and he tackled the project in a spirit of experimentation.

We held a ceremonial ground-breaking on July 14, 2006, and in less than six months Gavelle and his team of construction workers and engineers had created the factory. Just 7,500 square feet in size, it is small but highly efficient as well as eco-friendly. It contains water treatment equipment, recycling facilities, and a biogas unit that converts natural waste into energy, as well as solar panels to minimize the impact on the environment.

Pleased with his work, Gavelle pronounced the new factory "cute." He trained a team of Bangladeshi workers to run the plant, teaching them the high production, safety, and purity standards by which Danone operates around the world. It was important that the Bogra plant be ready to run without outside supervision once Gavelle had completed the project and moved on to his next international assignment.

As the plant was being built, other important business decisions were being made. Nutritionists, food production experts, and marketing specialists were working closely with local people from Bangladesh to test varying recipes for the yogurt. Eventually a formula was developed that used date molasses (a Bangladeshi product) as a sweetener. It also contained an array of the micronutrients Bangladeshi children desperately needed for good health, including vitamin A, iron, calcium, zinc, and iodine. In fact, a single serving provided 30 percent of a child's daily requirements of these crucial nutrients. Children from the area around Bogra happily gobbled samples of the yogurt and asked for more.

A local supply network for the ingredients was also planned. Ninety percent of the milk market in Bangladesh is operated on what's called an "informal" basis. In other words, farmers simply haul their milk on carts to local marketplaces or sell it to their friends, family, and neighbors.

This "backward" marketplace for milk could have made it very difficult for Grameen Danone to secure a reliable supply of raw material. Here is where our deep roots in the country's rural economy came in handy. Back in 2000, Grameen Bank had helped to found the Grameen Fisheries and Livestock Foundation, a network of local farmers who receive microcredit, animal insurance, veterinary services, and agricultural training. Grameen Danone was able to contract with the foundation as a steady source of milk supplies.

And as with any new consumer product, Grameen Danone had to give thought to marketing and sales. The company came up with the name Shokti Doi, which in the Bengali language means "yogurt for energy." Based on the results of a survey among local children, it chose a lion as the mascot to symbolize the product. An artist designed a friendly-looking cartoon lion, flexing his muscles, to adorn the lid of the Grameen Danone container. This character quickly became a favorite among the local kids.

The yogurt was priced at 5 taka for an eighty-gram cup. That's the equivalent of about 7 cents in American currency. By contrast, locally produced yogurt from the shops in Bogra traditionally sold for the equivalent of 30 cents a cup—not much money by Western standards, but too much for many rural Bangladeshi families. The goal, of course, was to get our nutrition-packed yogurt into the hands of as many poor people as possible.

In February 2007, the first commercial packages of Shokti Doi rolled off the production line in Bogra. It was an exciting, hopeful moment for the members of the Grameen Danone team.

And then things began to get interesting.

If at First You Don't Succeed. . . .

Over the first several months the Bogra plant was in operation, everything seemed to go smoothly. The equipment ran well, the yogurt was creamy and delicious, and most people who tried it liked it. But sales didn't grow very fast. Grameen Danone spent the months of spring and summer 2007 trying to figure out why.

Grameen Danone relied on a "two-legged stool" to distribute and sell Shokti Doi. One leg was a number of small retail stores located in and around Bogra. It's a fairly large city, with a population of over 100,000 in the city itself and a couple hundred thousand more in the neighboring areas (within around thirty kilometers, or twenty miles, of the city). But the number of stores in which Shokti Doi could be sold was fairly small, between three hundred and four hundred. The reason is that yogurt requires refrigeration, and district towns in Bangladesh, even in a city like Bogra, do not enjoy reliable electrical service. However, Grameen Danone did its best to promote the product to shop owners, and within a few months it was widely available in small stores in and around Bogra.

The second leg of Grameen Danone's sales operation was the "Grameen ladies." These are female entrepreneurs who have taken loans from Grameen Bank and used the money to start or expand small businesses with which to support themselves and their families. The Grameen ladies run all kinds of businesses—tending small vegetable plots, raising poultry and livestock, weaving baskets, selling clothing, making dresses, and so on. As I mentioned earlier, some are also "phone ladies," who use their Grameen loans to buy cell phones with which they provide telephone service on a per-call basis to neighbors who don't have their own phones.

When we launched Grameen Danone, we believed the Grameen ladies would form an important sales network for our yogurt. Grameen Danone recruited a number of our borrowers from around Bogra, gave them training lessons about the benefits of Shokti Doi, and provided them with insulated bags in which to carry the yogurt containers from door to door. Grameen Danone planned to pay a sales commission of one-half taka per cup sold. Grameen Danone's thinking was that an effective saleswoman might be able to sell enough yogurt to earn up to a few hundred taka per month—a significant extra income for a rural Bangladeshi family.

But during the early months of 2007, sales by the Grameen ladies were small. Grameen Danone's recruitment efforts failed to gain traction. Sometimes women would sign on to the program, sell yogurt for a few days, then quit without a word of explanation. As a result, Grameen Danone never had more than thirty saleswomen visiting their neighbors with the yogurt.

This meant that, between the shops in Bogra and the saleswoman network, sales of Shokti Doi seemed to be stuck at around 3,000 cups per day. It wasn't enough to make our beautiful factory self-sustaining, and certainly not enough to make the nutritional impact we were hoping for.

In the late summer of 2007, two things happened that moved Grameen Danone off the starting point where it seemed stuck.

First, the company tried to understand the problem and had discussions with Grameen staff and NGOs. The local experts they consulted with gave this advice: "The problem is with your management." And they explained:

> You do some things right. You select the ladies, train them about the yogurt, and then send them out into the field to sell. But you do not coach them properly about selling technique. What's more important, you fail to involve the woman's entire community. In Bangladesh, a woman is never an isolated being, living and working for herself. She is part of a family. If you want to create a successful partnership with her, you must get to know the family as well—especially her husband.
>
> This is particularly true when you are talking about door-to-door selling. In Bangladeshi rural culture, women tend to stay close to home. It is hard for them to step outside the confines of the home without the support of the men in their lives. Most of the ladies who take loans from Grameen Bank operate businesses at home—growing food, weaving cloth, making baskets. But selling door-to-door is a different matter. If the husband does not approve, the wife will feel unable to keep such a job.

This was an eye-opening moment for the Grameen Danone team. They realized that a cultural barrier had prevented them from working most effectively with the village ladies—a barrier that was all the stronger for being unspoken.

The second good thing that happened during the summer of 2007 was hiring a full-time managing director of Grameen Danone. Selecting a local manager steeped in the culture of the community was a big step toward making Grameen Danone into a company the village people could understand and support.

Under the new leadership, the process for recruiting, selecting, and training saleswomen was completely revamped. Grameen Danone took care to involve the women's families, especially their husbands, and to make sure that each saleswoman had her community's support behind her. As a result, the number of saleswomen grew steadily, from just 29 in September 2007 to 270 by the following March.

In addition, Grameen Danone made a minor adjustment to the yogurt recipe. Customers had been complaining that Grameen Danone yogurt was not sweet enough. In response, Grameen Danone added a little more molasses flavoring. (Grameen Danone yogurt is still not quite as sweet as the traditional product sold on the streets of Bogra, however.)

The benefits of all these changes soon became apparent. After seven months of basically stagnant sales, October 2007 saw the biggest sales increase in Grameen Danone's brief history. November was even better, and December was better still. In fact, between October 2007 and March 2008, Grameen Danone experienced six consecutive months of sales improvement. Monthly yogurt sales soared during this period.

This sales increase came almost entirely from Grameen Danone's rapidly growing rural sales network. The Grameen ladies sales model the company had envisioned from the beginning of the project appeared to be taking shape. Even more encouraging, a study Grameen Danone did during the winter of 2007 indicated that in the villages where the sales network was most fully developed, between 40 percent and 50 percent of the children were eating Shokti Doi. This high sales penetration made Grameen Danone optimistic that the nutritional benefits it had hoped to provide the children of Bangladesh were quite realistic.

But even as Grameen Danone's sales and marketing efforts were achieving success, events in the larger world were beginning to have a serious impact on the company.

Responding to a Global Crisis

Beginning as early as 2006, global food prices had begun to rise steadily. There were several causes for this increase. They included:

- Unseasonable droughts affecting grain production in such major wheat-exporting countries as Australia and the United States
- Population growth and expanding affluence in developing nations like India and China, which increased demand both for basic foods and for the more expensive meat products that, in turn, depend on grains and other animal feeds
- Increases in the price of oil and other petroleum products, which led to higher prices for shipping farm products as well as increased costs for petroleum-based fertilizers
- The growing use of wheat and corn to make ethanol fuel (especially in the United States), which produces artificial shortages of those foods

Because of the spread of free trade policies over the past two decades, the world has become, for most practical purposes, a single agricultural market. This means that price trends in one marketplace eventually affect every country. So as prices for grains and other food products rose in the developed world during 2006 and 2007, similar increases occurred in the developing nations, including Bangladesh.

For many Americans, an increase in the price of food is merely an inconvenience. For people in the poor nations of the Global South, it is often the difference between life and death. The year 2007 saw a dramatic increase in the number of people suffering from hunger around the world. Headlines and cable TV news footage of "food riots" in countries from Mexico and Cameroon to Senegal and Pakistan conveyed the seriousness of the problem.

In Bangladesh, the problem was exacerbated by two consecutive years of worse-than-normal flooding during the monsoon season (June

to October). This yearly inundation is normally a benign event, leading to the extraordinary fertility of our lush farmlands. But when nature produces a more extreme version of the seasonal rainfalls, farms
and villages are swept away, causing terrible hardship, homelessness,
and many deaths. It's a problem that we fear will be made much worse
by the growing impact of global warming and the rising ocean levels
it is producing.

For Grameen Danone, all these trends combined to create a serious
challenge to its business model. Along with the price of rice and meat,
the price of milk—the most important ingredient in yogurt—doubled.
The higher cost of raw materials completely ate up the small profit
margin Grameen Danone had established when pricing its product. In
fact, by the time sales reached their then-peak level in March 2008,
Grameen Danone was actually losing money on every cup of yogurt it
sold. Obviously this was not a sustainable way of doing business.

But how to respond to this challenge? That wasn't so clear. The
Grameen Danone board, including representatives from both Groupe
Danone and Grameen—French business experts and Bangladeshi experts on rural women and children—wrestled with the problem for
more than two months.

There were two schools of thought on the board. One group insisted that Grameen Danone had to raise the price of the yogurt to
cover the new, higher costs. Grameen Danone is a social business, not
a charity. Of course, it is important to provide the nutritional benefits
to its poor customers in a form they can afford. But if Grameen
Danone loses money every month, there is no way it can stay in business. If mounting losses eventually cause Grameen Danone to shut its
doors, the benefits to the poor will disappear forever. So maintaining
low prices that are artificial and unsustainable is *not* going to help the
poor in the long run.

The other side of the debate said that keeping Grameen Danone's
established price of 5 taka for an eighty-gram cup was necessary to
maintain the growth of its still-new business. Those who advocated

this course said, "Changing the price of a product that is still in the launch phase could be a fatal mistake. Rather than increase the cost of the yogurt, Grameen Danone needs to find a way to reduce its expenses. Otherwise Grameen Danone may drive away the customers, perhaps permanently."

The debate raged between Paris and Dhaka for several weeks. Both sides raised smart, thoughtful arguments. I was among those who supported increasing the price of the yogurt.

I strongly believe that a social business must be managed on a sustainable basis from day one. It's a mistake to establish prices, procedures, or business methods that are not realistic in the early months of the business.

Such a course is courting disaster. It means that your customers, suppliers, and employees will all become accustomed to an economic structure that simply does not work. When the time comes that you are forced to change direction—as it almost surely will—you run the risk of alienating everyone whose good will you rely on.

So mine was one of the voices urging that the price of a cup of Shokti Doi be increased as necessary to cover the costs. And in the end, this plan was adopted. In April 2008, Grameen Danone raised the price for an eighty-gram cup from 5 taka to 8 taka.

At the same time, the company rejected a second proposal—that it alter the method by which saleswomen were paid. Rather than continue to pay on commission, these members suggested, Grameen Danone should offer a fixed salary, regardless of their sales volume. The idea was that if yogurt sales fell dramatically as a result of the price increase, the women would be shielded from the impact. This was proposed as both a humane thing to do and also a way of keeping the sales network intact even in the face of falling sales volume.

The Grameen Danone board voted against this plan for the same reason it decided to raise the prices. The board was determined to run Grameen Danone on a sustainable basis. Paying a salary that was not justified by the sales the women produced would transform the company into a form of charity. The board didn't want to abandon the social business model at this, its first moment of crisis.

So Grameen Danone went ahead with the price increase. And the results were devastating.

First, sales plummeted. Grameen Danone lost around 80 percent of its sales in the rural areas—understandably so, since its customers, already hit hard by the global economic crisis, were simply unable to afford a product whose price had just risen by 60 percent. (Urban sales through small shops in and around Bogra were also affected, though not as greatly; city dwellers are somewhat more affluent than rural people, so the decline in store sales was "only" around 40 percent.)

Second, the rural sales network Grameen Danone had built so painstakingly over the previous six months collapsed. With their customers disappearing, the saleswomen abandoned the business. Soon Grameen Danone had no way to reach its rural customers, even if any of them still wanted to buy the product. An 80 percent sales decline turned into a complete washout.

Grameen Danone's business was now a year old, and it was back at square one. It was time to rethink the plan from the bottom up.

Fortunately, it now had a year's experience and learning to build on, as well as the leadership of a solid managerial team. This team began to examine all of the assumptions of its business, starting with the product itself.

It was clear that the sudden, sharp increase in price from 5 to 8 taka had been too much of a shock for the rural market. Grameen Danone realized it had to develop a more affordable version of the product.

The Danone food-development experts set to work. They'd doubted whether it would be possible to maintain the same level of micronutrients in a good-tasting yogurt if the size of a serving shrank below eighty grams. Now they conducted further experiments using the slightly sweeter recipe and found that they could pack the same nutrients, representing 30 percent of a child's daily requirements, into a sixty-gram container.

It was a smaller snack, yes, but no smaller than the serving sold by Danone in other countries, such as Turkey. So in June 2008, this became the new standard yogurt package for the rural market—sixty grams priced at 6 taka, just 1 taka higher than the original price.

The board supported the launch of this new, reformulated package with a series of small promotional events and school nutrition programs in the villages. Gradually Grameen Danone began rebuilding its ladies' network. Soon the company had a new, smaller, but very effective team of thirty-five ladies working seventeen days a month and selling around fifty cups per day each, for a total of almost 30,000 cups a month in rural sales—not a bad basis from which to grow.

Grameen Danone also realized that it was important to continue to grow the city market, using refrigerated food shops. This was a financial necessity. Its current sales level utilized only a small fraction of the total capacity of the Bogra plant, which was inherently inefficient and costly. Increasing sales volume would reduce the per-unit cost and bring Grameen Danone much closer to the break-even point. And in the short run, the most practical way to do so was to sell more yogurt in the towns.

Grameen Danone advanced on two fronts. First, it expanded the retail store program to include two smaller cities, Rajshahi and Pabna, each about fifty kilometers (around thirty miles) outside Bogra. (Previously sales had been restricted to a thirty-kilometer, or roughly twenty-mile, radius from that city.) In these "local city" stores, the eighty-gram container is sold for 8 taka, which appears to be affordable for urban customers.

Second, it worked to accelerate plans for a strategic move that had always been contemplated—namely, to make the yogurt available in Bangladesh's largest city, Dhaka.

This required a more significant change in the business plan. Specifically, it called for the creation of a distribution center with a refrigerated warehouse and the outfitting of a refrigerated truck to carry yogurt supplies from the Bogra factory to Dhaka twice a week, a three-hour drive. The maintenance of a "cold chain" to keep the yogurt fresh and maintain its optimal flavor is a costly requirement that Grameen Danone had sought to avoid through its original "hyperlocal" marketing plan. But now, with the pressing need to boost sales volume to improve margins, Grameen Danone decided to make the investment.

To cover the higher delivery cost, Grameen Danone set the price of an eighty-gram cup for Dhaka at 12 taka. That's a price that village customers would find unacceptably high, but that city residents would be able and willing to pay. Starting in November 2008, Grameen Danone began to build up a network of shops in Dhaka (where refrigeration is almost universal) that wanted to carry the yogurt. Soon Grameen Danone had a large and growing number of city neighborhoods where Shokti Doi was available.

The Winning Formula?

Today, as a result of Grameen Danone's experiments and changes in direction, its business model appears to be working. The company serves a two-part market, urban and rural, using systems and even products that are distinctly different.

In the cities, including Bogra, Dhaka, and the surrounding towns, Grameen Danone sells its yogurt through a network of more than 1,600 shops. The company has created a beachhead in Bangladesh's second city, Chittagong (which happens to be my hometown). So far, just a handful of shops in Chittagong carry the yogurt, but in time, their number will grow.

Grameen Danone has also begun to diversify its product offerings to appeal to even more customers (adults as well as children), boost its sales volume, and increase the utilization of its Bogra factory. Grameen Danone has a new flavor of yogurt—mango—as well as an affordably priced yogurt drink. Containers of mango yogurt sell for 7 taka for sixty grams and 12 taka for eighty grams, while the drink is available in a fifty-milliliter container, priced at 5 taka, and a seventy-milliliter container, priced at 7 taka.

To reflect this expanding lineup of products, the company introduced a new brand name. As of September 2008, all Grameen Danone products carry the name Shokti + (that is, "energy plus"). By dropping the word "yogurt" from the brand name, Grameen Danone is increasing its freedom to expand into other products in the future—for example, baby food, which is one of Danone's most successful product lines in other parts of the world. Grameen Danone may or may not add such products to its lineup in the near future, but by using the Shokti + brand name, the company has the option of doing so whenever it makes business sense.

Meanwhile, the rural sales network in the Bogra region continues to grow. Today, around 175 saleswomen sell the yogurt through a variety of channels. Some go door to door in their local village, others sell from small shops in their homes, and still others visit the weekly meetings of Grameen Bank branch centers, where they sell the yogurt to the women and children who attend.

Typically the saleswoman buys the sixty-gram containers from the factory at 5 taka each, sells them for 6 taka, and keeps the 1-taka difference as her commission. Since the average saleswoman distributes around fifty containers per day and works four days each week, she probably grosses around 800 taka per month, roughly the equivalent of $11. For a rural woman in Bangladesh, this is a meaningful supplement to her family's income.

Thanks to this two-pronged sales and marketing approach, the business now appears to be on a powerful growth track. Between 30 percent and 40 percent of Grameen Danone sales are now in the city of Dhaka. Grameen Danone thinks these represent only the tip of the iceberg; in a city with a population of over 12 million, there's almost no limit to the amount of yogurt Grameen Danone can sell. And the company has increased its use of the Bogra factory to full capacity, which is a big achievement.

The next important milestone will be the break-even point, at which Grameen Danone revenues will cover its expenses. Soon thereafter, Grameen Danone will begin to generate a surplus, which can be invested in expanding the business. Grameen Danone expects to achieve this sometime during 2010—but as the experience in the past two years has demonstrated, in today's unpredictable economic environment, almost anything can happen.

Looking back, it's easy to see that the milk-price increase of 2007–2008 and the sales collapse that occurred when Grameen Danone raised the price of its yogurt to cover it represented a business crisis that might have seriously damaged the business. Was it a mistake to raise the price? Perhaps so—but keeping the lower, unsustainable price was not a viable option. What I wish I had known was that a third alternative existed: to reformulate the product and create a smaller, more affordable package, as Grameen Danone ultimately did.

Thankfully, Grameen Danone came up with this creative solution in time to save the company and set it on the path to new growth. Perhaps the next time Grameen Danone faces a similar crisis it will remember what happened and respond to it even more sure-footedly.

Lessons from Three Tumultuous Years

In *Creating a World Without Poverty*, I wrote, "A social business must be *at least* as well-managed as any profit-maximizing business." Our experience with Grameen Danone has certainly demonstrated the truth of that statement. The challenge of creating Grameen Danone has not been made any easier by its status as a social business—if anything, just the opposite has been true.

It is quite difficult to design a business that generates strong and growing sales of a useful product, so that the business can sustain itself. It is also quite difficult to design an organization that provides a clear, measurable benefit to society or to a significant segment of society—for example, better nutrition for the poor. It is even *more* difficult to design a social business that does both things at the same time.

In that previous book, I also quoted the words of the famous architect Ludwig Mies van der Rohe: "God is in the details." Those words have also proven to be very applicable to the Grameen Danone story. In building the success of the business, the company leaders had to pay close attention to a host of details, adjusting and changing their plans as dictated by circumstances, thinking carefully and continually about how small details have a big effect on Grameen Danone's sales and on the success of the entire enterprise.

Here are some of the many lessons learned during the first three years in the history of Grameen Danone. I think others who are interested in launching social businesses of their own will find them useful.

Be flexible, yet never lose sight of your central goal. As you've seen, it was necessary to make many changes in the business design—despite the fact that Grameen Danone spent months in thoughtful analysis and planning before it ever broke ground for the factory or produced a single cup of yogurt. Life is just too complicated for anyone, no matter how farsighted, to predict every contingency.

So don't be afraid to adjust your business plan when circumstances make it necessary. But to avoid becoming purely reactive, flitting from one program to the next, always remember the central goal for which you established the social business in the first place.

In the case of Grameen Danone, that goal was to bring better nutrition to the people of Bangladesh, especially the children. Any change in its business plan that would make it easier to achieve that goal would be a good one; any change that would divert or distract it from that goal would be a bad one. This touchstone made it possible for the company to choose among various alternatives throughout its early months. Would shifting more of its sales and marketing efforts to the cities rather than the countryside be a wise decision? Yes—because it would help the company put its nutritious product in the hands of more people than would otherwise be possible.

Immerse yourself in the culture of the people you intend to serve. As every businessperson knows, understanding your customer is one of the indispensable keys to success. And this means, among other things, understanding and empathizing with the culture of the people you serve: their values, dreams, desires, fears, aversions, likes, and dislikes.

This is even more important when you are trying to build a social business. Those who want to offer a social benefit to people in their community are sometimes prone to arrogance. They are "do-gooders" with fine intentions who want to make the world a better place. As a result, they can be impatient with the "blind spots," weaknesses, failings, or flaws of their "clients," and even of their simple cultural differences. If, as a social business entrepreneur, you sometimes find yourself wondering, "What's the matter with these people? Why don't they appreciate the good things I am trying to do for them?" it's a sign you are wandering down the wrong path. Stop and rethink your plan!

Cultural misunderstandings can occur even when the people you are serving are well-known to you, as we found when we struggled to create an effective rural sales force for Shokti Doi. Remember that when people are thrust into a new situation or confronted with a new challenge, they are likely to behave differently than you expect. They are not "right" or "wrong," just different—and if you want to serve them effectively, the quicker you figure out what really makes them tick, the better the results will be.

Use help from allies wherever you may find them. Grameen Danone owes its very existence to a partnership between unlikely allies— Grameen Bank, a unique rural finance institution for the poor, and Groupe Danone, a wealthy consumer products company from France. Yet our two organizations have proven to be highly compatible thanks to our shared values and our different yet complementary business skills. Grameen Danone could never have been created without Franck Riboud, Emmanuel Faber, and their many able executives, nor could Groupe Danone have connected so well with the rural Bangladesh market without Grameen's network.

I think this is how social businesses everywhere are likely to work. As I've often said, human beings have a natural desire to help one another. It's a motivating force that is just as powerful as the desire for profit. Social business taps and satisfies this desire to do good. Therefore, those who are building social businesses should not be surprised when they encounter people in unlikely places who want to help—nor should they be shy about accepting the support when it is offered.

Take advantage of differing opportunities in different markets. As we've emphasized, it's important for a social business to be financially self-sustaining. Grameen Danone is well on its way to achieving that goal. But this might not be the case if it had insisted on seeing all its potential customers through the same lens.

At Grameen Bank, our exclusive experience is with rural poor women. (Actually, under the terms of our government charter, our bank is permitted to operate only in the countryside, not in the cities.) And since the worst problems of poverty and malnutrition in Bangladesh exist in rural areas, and among the poor, Grameen Danone was launched with the intention of serving mainly a rural market, distributing its product in the city only after establishing a strong foothold in the country, if at all.

In practice, however, Grameen Danone has found that the best approach is to tackle both markets simultaneously—but not in the same way. In the city, it can sell yogurt at a price that is slightly higher (though still affordable to the urban poor), building sales and production volume while generating profits to subsidize the less-affluent rural market. The ability to quickly build a strong base of urban sales is giving the company time to address the more difficult long-term challenge of building a rural sales network, one village and district at a time.

Actually, we at Grameen had always intended to use cross-subsidization as part of our path to financial stability. We'd already used the same approach to make our eye hospital economically sustainable, so we knew it worked. But in the early days, the Danone people were not ready to do it. It took time for our partners to be ready to understand and support this concept. In social business, as in other kinds of business, patience is often a necessary ingredient! "The readiness is all," as Shakespeare wrote.

Now cross-subsidization appears to be working. Though very different, the two markets support one another and work together to make Grameen Danone a stronger, more sustainable business. I believe a similar dynamic is likely to exist in many social businesses in countries around the world.

Question your own assumptions. Even ideas you've developed through long experience and careful study may need to be challenged from time to time. When formulating the product, Danone's world-class team of nutritional experts concluded that a serving of eighty grams was needed to serve as a carrier for the high dose of micronutrients we wanted to deliver. Anything less, they feared, would let the nutritional supplements give the yogurt an "off" taste that would make children reject it.

Not until the milk price crisis forced the company to reexamine this assumption did it discover that it was wrong, and that a smaller, less-expensive serving of yogurt could pack the same nutritional punch.

If you are trying to build a social business, you should periodically look back at the assumptions you've made—the alternatives you ruled out, or the choices you felt you *had* to make—and consider whether they are still valid. You may find that circumstances have changed or that your initial beliefs were simply wrong—which may open up new opportunities you never dreamed existed.

Seed Money From a Social Business Fund

In the long run, what may be as exciting as the story of Grameen Danone itself is the story of Danone Communities. This is an investment fund launched by Groupe Danone that is the source of the initial monies used to create Grameen Danone. In the years to come, Danone Communities will also be a source of investment money for other social businesses.

All the money invested by Danone Communities comes from Danone shareholders and employees who choose to contribute to the fund using income from their work. These investors knew they would not receive a market return on their money. When the fund was created, investors were told that they would get back the money they invested, but no interest, dividends, or capital gains beyond a nominal return of 1 percent. In addition, 10 percent of the fund's money would be invested in social businesses that would not give any profit at all. Nonetheless, they chose to contribute to Danone Communities rather than to another, more lucrative investment fund because of the personal satisfaction they derived from knowing that their money was going to create businesses that would benefit humankind.

I always felt uncomfortable about the fact that our agreement with Danone inadvertently included a clause promising a 1 percent dividend for investment in Grameen Danone. As I mentioned in *Creating a World Without Poverty,* this was a mistake which I blame on the speed at which we hurried the whole signing process. Afterward, I kept reminding Emmanuel Faber that the agreement had to be corrected, and he always assured me that it would be done.

In December 2009, a board meeting of Grameen Danone was held in Dhaka, with Emmanuel Faber and a number of other Danone senior executives in attendance. At this meeting, Faber proudly announced that the Danone Communities Fund was ready to amend the shareholders' agreement to eliminate the 1 percent dividend. The fund would be happy to receive back its initial investment, with no dividend beyond that. I was extremely happy to hear the announcement. "What a relief!" I thought. "Finally, the day has come!"

Everyone in the room burst out in cheering and applause when this announcement was made. Someone remarked, "This is the first time in business history that owners are celebrating because a dividend payment has been waived!" It's the first time—but I predict it will not be the last.

The next day, Faber sent me the following e-mail:

> Dear Yunus,
> It has been a renewed pleasure to work with you yesterday. . . . I will remember this UNIQUE moment in the history of modern capitalism of a corporate board where members applaud and congratulate each other for having definitely succeeded in avoiding any risk of receiving any dividend in the future!!! Cheers!!!!
> Best,
> Em

I find it impressive not only that fully one-third of Danone employees have chosen to place a portion of their income into the Danone Communities Fund, but also that they have agreed to eliminate even the modest 1 percent dividend that was agreed upon in the legal document. The investors in Grameen Danone now know that their sole benefit is the psychological and spiritual one of helping poor people halfway around the world. It's a remarkable sign of support for this new and unproven, but very important, investment concept.

A Great Beginning in 2010

The year 2010 started off with several pieces of good news for Grameen Danone. The company crossed the 100-ton-per-month production level; it became operationally viable and is close to being financially viable;

and preparations are being made at full speed to launch the second plant this year. In the next few years, Grameen Danone hopes to make its products available in many of the major cities of Bangladesh. The second plant will be located near Dhaka, where the greatest opportunity exists. It will be a small plant similar to the one in Bogra. Guy Gavelle, Danone's gifted engineer/designer, has said he will be able to build this second plant at a cost that is 30 percent lower than even the highly efficient and economical plant he built in Bogra. It should go into production in 2010. Franck Riboud plans to attend the grand opening.

In the meantime, Grameen Danone is working to strengthen and expand its rural sales system in the Bogra area. The company wants to reach a point where every child who can benefit from the nutrients in Shokti + has a chance to enjoy the product. Then Grameen Danone will begin to apply the same sales and distribution system in other rural areas around the country. Eventually, the company expects to reach its goal of having around fifty factories throughout Bangladesh, serving the entire population of the country, down to the most remote villages.

This is similar to my experience with Grameen Bank. The initial challenge is to develop a model that works, to test and refine it, and to adjust it as necessary when conditions change. Then, when you've proven that the model is effective, you roll it out in one district after another. At every stage in the process, you need to keep a close eye on results and be prepared to make necessary changes, since methods that work in one place or at one time may need to be adapted for other circumstances. The challenges are very rewarding as well as endlessly fascinating.

Although in its brief history Grameen Danone has had more than its share of ups and downs, the experience has left me more convinced than ever of my belief in the potentially transformative power of social business, not just in Bangladesh but around the world.

CHAPTER 3

Launching a Social Business

S ocial business is a new idea. Yet the impulses that lie behind the creation of a social business are familiar to everyone. Creativity, entrepreneurship, and the desire to make the world a better place— these are feelings that millions of people share. And those feelings are all you need to want to start a social business.

Of course, we are accustomed to using the word "entrepreneurship" in a traditional business context. The main difference between starting a social business and starting a regular business is the core motivation of the entrepreneur. Like any entrepreneur, the creator of a social business is ambitious, energetic, and creative—a dreamer of big dreams. But in the social business realm, the entrepreneur's underlying drive is different. Most people who want to start a profit-maximizing business are focused on earning money—preferably a lot of money, because the amount of profit is the yardstick by which success is measured. So they start the search for an idea by looking for a powerful business case—a market of customers with money to spend who are underserved; a product or service niche that no other company is filling; and a new way to supply a need for which lots of people are willing to pay top dollar.

But when you start a social business, you don't begin by looking for a business case that will generate maximum profits. Instead you pick a social problem you want to solve and then seek the business solution for it.

Profit is important only as a necessary condition, not as the ultimate goal. You are not trying to find the most profitable combination between a given market demand and your capabilities. The initial thought comes from somewhere else altogether: your human instinct of compassion. You may see or hear about a hardship people suffer and resolve to change it—a very natural response to the pain of others. Then you start looking for a solution. If you approach the project in a social business manner, you not only ensure your efforts will last, because they are economically sustainable by covering your costs, but you will also give those you help the dignity and self-respect of being a vital part of the global economic system rather than mere wards of charity.

So to start a social business, first identify a need and match it with your capabilities and talents. Look at the world around you and ask what disturbs you. What do you really want to change? Identify the root cause of the problem—what is the crucial need that needs to be addressed? Be precise, and dig deep rather than merely looking at the surface.

You can start by listing the problems of the world. You could easily fill up a whole notebook listing these problems. Pick any one of them and ask yourself, "Can I design a social business to solve this problem?" That's the beginning. And when you go through your list of problems crying out for solutions, don't be discouraged because some of them demand things that "cannot be done." Those may be the very things that your unique talents have equipped you to do.

Use your creativity. Today we are lucky because any small creativity can be magnified into big creativity through the power of technology. Tomorrow even more powerful technologies will be available. Things that you cannot believe today will happen tomorrow. How to use that technology to address social problems is the great challenge— and the great opportunity—for social business.

Many problems are waiting to be solved: poverty, hunger, disease, healthcare, unemployment, abandoned children, drugs, housing, pollution, environment, and so on. Look at your own neighborhood to see which are the pressing problems near you. Make a list of general headings of the issues you want to explore further. Under each general heading see which specific things could be turned into a social business, and start working on one such item. Build a business plan around it by gathering information on various aspects of this business.

The right problem to choose is the one you can handle with ease. Don't go for a highly ambitious business or the most important problem you can imagine when designing your first undertaking. Instead seek out a good learning ground. You may get involved with many social businesses in the future. But for now you are just learning the basics of setting up and running a social business.

Start where you are, making use of whatever skills, resources, and other advantages you already have. And where there is a disconnect between the problem you want to address and the resources you have, use your ingenuity to forge a connection.

For example, you may be worried about the poor people of the developing world: countries in Africa, South Asia, Latin America. Yet you may be far from the workers, farmers, and craftsmen of the developing world, in Europe, Japan, or North America. You may never even have traveled to the nations of the South. Then what can you do? Take advantage of what you know. You know your home market, the people around you; you know how to create a particular good or service; you have a particular set of skills that are unique to you. So think about your social business in a flexible way. In every business, there are people involved along the entire value chain—from the farming to the processing, the manufacturing, the selling, and ultimately the buying of the product—and there are poor people in every country. Find the group you can help first, possibly in a developed country. Later you can expand your efforts to bring in more beneficiaries. Do not get disheartened. Start where you are.

As long as you are confident that you can sell your product and fulfill the objective of your social business, go ahead. It may not be the most celebrated social business, but it is a social business. The important thing is to make it a success. If you devise a highly ambitious social business plan and then struggle with it for months and years with no success, you won't feel good about it.

Don't let that happen to you. You must enjoy your social business. One of the basic principles we strive to uphold is "Do it with joy!" Don't forget that motto. Live it every day.

As for defining the needs of the poor: Don't go into complicated arguments about what is in the minds of the poor, or about what sociological or economic studies have shown about the path out of poverty. Keep it simple. Everybody needs food, income, healthcare, housing, water, financial services, electricity, sanitation, information technology, and so on. If you can deliver anything related to these even in a small way, go ahead and do it. And if anyone can make your undertaking easier, enlist their help.

Next, clarify your objective to make absolutely sure you get the desired result from the project. Then come up with a product or service to serve as the vehicle for achieving this objective. Make sure the connection between the product and the objective is very clear.

Don't expect your first design of a social business to be a roaring success. First trials usually end up in failure. It's like putting a rocket into space. The space programs in the United States and the Soviet Union back in the 1960s and '70s involved many failures. Rockets exploded on their launching pads. But each failure represented a step on the road to ultimate success. Finally, in 1969, the entire world watched as an astronaut took the first step on the surface of the moon. This is how experiments work.

Similarly, if you design something, don't expect it to fly right away. It will need a little fixing here, and a little fixing there; it will go up, but it will come down again. Keep on trying. Have faith in your creativity

Someday it will fly. That's what creativity is all about. You don't give up. You start out with an idea, and you keep trying until it works.

From a Grand Objective to a Specific Goal

Don't get so caught up in grand dreams that you overlook opportunities to begin doing good right away. Instead, find ways to translate those grand dreams into specific, concrete goals.

For example, eradicating poverty is a grand social objective. How will you pursue it?

I can give you some hints about how to go about it. You can say, "I can provide employment to, say, five poor people." How will you create jobs for them? There are a thousand and one ways to create jobs. In fact, practically any successful social business can do just that. If you create a social business, you do so for the sake of creating jobs, not for the sake of making money for yourself. You will have solved the problem of poverty—not for the whole world, but for your first five beneficiaries because you created jobs for them. So you can eradicate poverty—at least on a small scale—by creating a social business.

Microfinance is another form of social business that can eradicate poverty. You can provide microcredit to poor people so they can create their own jobs through self-employment. That is another way to eradicate poverty—one person at a time.

Suppose your background, experience, knowledge, and interests lead you to think about healthcare as a possible field in which to launch a social business. Don't start by trying to reform the world healthcare system. Instead, think about the hundreds of smaller opportunities that exist in the universe of healthcare. Try to split the problem up into manageable pieces. Take one piece and build an independent social business out of it.

This is exactly what we are doing with our joint venture partners in Bangladesh. Access to pure, safe drinking water is a health issue—so working with Veolia Water, we've created a social business to address it. Nutrition for poor children in the villages is a health issue—so we've partnered with Danone to address it through a social business. Lack of footwear makes millions of people in Bangladesh susceptible to diseases spread by parasites—so we're collaborating with adidas on a plan to create a social business that will offer shoes at the lowest possible price. Providing affordable cataract operations for poor people is a health issue—so we've launched two hospitals, operated as social businesses, that specialize in eye care, particularly cataract operations. The global problem of healthcare is too big to tackle all at once—so we've broken it up into smaller pieces and are addressing those pieces individually.

Within the broad category of healthcare, we are now moving forward on several more fronts. There is a big shortage of nurses in Bangladesh—and in the world. This problem is an opportunity for us. We have 8 million families who are Grameen Bank borrowers. Plenty of young women in these families could qualify to go to nursing colleges, if only nursing colleges were available. So we thought, "Why don't we set up nursing colleges and give these young women student loans from Grameen Bank?" The nursing colleges will make enough money from tuition and fees to cover their costs—a classic social business model.

We will offer each of these women a guaranteed job. As soon as she gets her nursing degree, she will have a job with Grameen Healthcare at an attractive starting salary of 15,000 taka per month ($220). Out of this salary, she will pay one-third as a loan installment until the loan is paid off. These nurses can get international jobs too, paying a salary upward of 70,000 taka ($1,000) per month.

Notice what is happening here. Each small piece of the healthcare problem that we are addressing with an individual social business is beginning to contribute to an overall solution to the healthcare problems of Bangladesh as a whole. Better nutrition for kids and pure drinking water in the villages will reduce the incidence of preventable diseases, reducing the strain on hospitals and clinics. Affordable shoes for rural people will protect them from parasitic diseases. Opening nursing colleges will create a stream of trained professionals who can bring better healthcare to millions in the country, as well as producing incomes that will reduce poverty and thereby improve the health status of many more people. As we add more pieces to the puzzle, the entire picture will continue to improve. A downward spiral has been transformed into an upward spiral—not by creating a massive "grand plan" for fixing the system, but by improving one piece at a time.

There are still many more opportunities for new social businesses in the healthcare sphere—not only in Bangladesh and other countries of the developing world, but everywhere.

Making prescription drugs affordable for everybody is a great social business opportunity. In many cases the price of medicine is too high. The real cost of production may be modest, but the producers spend a lot of money to put the drugs in very attractive packaging, and they spend more on marketing and public relations. Ultimately the patients have to pay for all these expenses. A social business dedicated to distributing medications at affordable prices could avoid all these extra expenses and lower the cost of the medicine for patients.

Obviously there are many important elements of such a business that need to be devised. Low-cost generic medicines can be provided at near-cost to poor people in Africa or South Asia. Questions will be raised by interested parties about the quality of the cheap medicine; regulators will be concerned. There will be other business difficulties to be resolved. But are they too difficult to overcome? I don't think so.

Providing vaccines could also be an attractive social business. Several vaccines in the world are very effective in protecting people from such common diseases as cholera, typhoid, and so on. But some of these vaccines are not produced by companies because the return on their investment is not high enough. There are six diseases known as orphan diseases because production of the vaccine is very low or nonexistent, despite the fact that people keep dying. The incidence of cholera, for example, is quite high in Bangladesh—yet the disease could be virtually eliminated through a vaccine that has already been proven effective.

There's nothing to stop anyone who is interested from launching a social business to produce and sell vaccines at an affordable price for the developing world. Two or three pieces of the supply chain would need to be developed: a production company to license the vaccine formulas and manufacture the vaccines; a marketing and distribution company to import the vaccines into the poor countries; and a company to sell supplies of vaccines to healthcare providers in cities and villages. From an economic perspective, cross-subsidization would probably be key to making this system sustainable. That is to say, middle-class people would be charged somewhat more than the cost of the vaccines to produce profits that could keep the charges to poor people at rock bottom—just a few cents per vaccine, if possible.

Again, there are challenges to be met in devising a workable plan for this business. But is it achievable? Every instinct in my body, based on decades of experience in creating businesses to serve the poor people of Bangladesh, tells me that it is.

A much longer list of healthcare opportunities for social business could be created. In many schools, lack of funding prevents the employment of a school nurse to provide routine first aid, preventive care, and health education—perhaps a social business could be created to staff every school with a trained nurse. Visiting healthcare professionals are badly needed to help elderly people, those with chronic diseases, and those who are too disabled to travel from their homes—there's no reason why such services couldn't be provided by a social business. Awareness of safe-sex practices can play a powerful role in preventing the spread of AIDS and other sexually transmitted diseases—why couldn't every neighborhood have a clinic, run as a social business, that would provide counseling and culturally appropriate training to young couples in how to protect themselves from such illnesses?

Start with a Personal Passion

If you are a physician, a nurse, a physical therapist, a drug researcher, or someone otherwise involved in the health field, you may already be excited to think about the many, many ways that healthcare could be transformed through the power of social business. But what if you work in a field that does not have any obvious application to the big social problems of our world—is it still possible to apply your talents to the challenges faced by humankind?

In many cases, the answer is a resounding yes. In fact, I strongly believe that with ingenuity, almost any personal passion can be transformed into a vehicle for making the world a better place.

Suppose you are involved in the world of culture—the arts, literature, music, dance, or theater. Is there any way to use your talents to create a powerful social business?

Certainly there is! My work with the Grameen companies has shown me time and again the important role that culture plays in shaping society. Cultural barriers often hold back social progress, while positive cultural forces can be used to promote enormous changes for the better.

In the early years of Grameen Bank, strong cultural norms in Bangladesh made it hard for us to attract female borrowers. Many women in the villages had never even touched money; some were actually afraid to enter a world they viewed as the exclusive province of men. Because they were mostly illiterate and largely sheltered from the communities in which they lived, many women were hesitant to take up the challenges that microcredit presented.

Over time, we solved these problems by creating a new, alternative culture for village ladies. We taught thousands to read and write, starting with their names—an incredibly empowering experience for them. Thousands more discovered the power of a shared community with other Grameen borrowers who supported one another. They learned to enjoy coming to the Grameen bank centers for weekly meetings at which they would sing songs, engage in simple exercises, and share stories about their families and the small businesses they had created.

Today, countless Grameen borrowers have become self-reliant, resourceful, daring women—a dramatic cultural change that has benefited not only them but their spouses, children, and communities.

This cultural change wasn't easy to create. People said we were destroying their culture; that women needed to be kept at home and that they weren't supposed to have, or handle, money. I said, "You keep your culture—I am creating a counter-culture."

Ever since then I have felt strongly that culture is useless unless it is constantly challenged by a counter-culture. People create culture; culture creates people. It is a two-way street. When people hide behind a culture, you know that's a dead culture, which is good for a museum but not good for human society. To experience progress, human society needs to move on, evolving and creating its own new culture step by step. We defied the dead culture in favor of a live culture that is dynamic and self-regenerating.

Today, we continue to face similar cultural challenges. For example, some villagers who are offered the chance to buy the fortified Shokti + yogurt don't understand its value or the importance of micronutrients for their children. "I was raised with just a cup of rice every day," they say. "Why isn't that good enough for my child?"

Here is one opportunity for a social business built around cultural offerings. Cultural programs like songs, dances, and plays could give the villagers of rural Bangladesh a better understanding of their families' health needs. Radio and television programs could be added to the mix. As more and more Bangladeshis obtain cell phones, cultural "apps" could be created to combine education, information, and entertainment. Such offerings could open up for millions of villagers the excitement of changing their lives.

So changing culture can be effectively done with cultural programs—and there is no reason such programs cannot be organized along social business lines.

Or suppose you are an engineer. Is there room for you in the world of social business?

Actually, the opportunities are almost unlimited. Here is one simple example: Why can't waste recycling be a very interesting social business?

Dhaka, the capital of Bangladesh, is like many of the rapidly growing cities of the developing world—plagued with unsanitary conditions caused by an influx of millions of poor people from the countryside, living in homes without proper sewage or garbage disposal systems. Yet this is a completely manageable problem—and one that lends itself to a beautiful social business. After all, waste is a valuable commodity. It can be converted into electricity, fertilizer, biofuel for cooking and heating, gas for powering vehicles—there are many possibilities. (I know this is true because Grameen Shakti, our renewable energy company, is already selling thousands of biogas plants based on recycled animal waste in rural Bangladesh.)

What's needed is for a smart civil engineer who has been bitten by the social business bug to set up shop in Dhaka—or perhaps in Tegucigalpa, Accra, Lagos, or some other city in the developing world—and create a social business that treats urban wastes in an economically and environmentally sustainable fashion. The model you develop can then be replicated across the globe, making life healthier and more enjoyable for millions of people.

What if you are a lover of the outdoors—a person who spends every free moment hiking, mountain climbing, or camping in the woods? Is there any way to make this the basis of a social business?

Absolutely. Consider the problem of global deforestation. Woodlands are being denuded all around the world by thoughtless individuals, greedy businesses, and in some cases government officials who are paid by the taxpayers to protect the forests. The destruction of forests is helping to accelerate climate change as well as making our planet a less beautiful home. Planting trees across huge tracts of land could be an excellent opportunity for social business.

Even a banker can find creative opportunities in social business—and I don't just mean in microcredit. Tens of millions of people around the world need better access to financial services, and every service that could be provided to them can be the basis for a successful social business.

One example: A social business in remittances would be an excellent idea. Many poor people depend on remittances as a crucial part of their economic lives. Poor workers travel across borders, and sometimes across oceans, to find work. Then they have to find a way to transfer their earnings to families at home who desperately need the money to survive. Unfortunately, poor people currently have to pay a lot every time they transfer their money. And this expense is needless, especially with the potential for modern information technology to handle such transfers electronically in a matter of seconds and at insignificant cost.

All that's required is for some smart banker—perhaps in partnership with an IT expert—to create an instant, low-cost remittances business. This is a very practical and sorely needed social business that could quickly improve the lives of countless people.

As you see, it really doesn't matter what kind of work you may have done before, what subject you specialized in at school, or what your particular talents are. Identify your special passion and find a way to link it to a problem someone is struggling with. Starting a social business should be fun, enjoyable, exciting, challenging, and fulfilling.

Building a Social Business Around People

If you are having trouble identifying a problem you want to solve, here is another approach: Look for a group of people who need help—then figure out how you can help them.

My work in Bangladesh is built around the many needs of the poor. You may choose to work with the poor as well, or you might identify some other group with important needs—the elderly, the disabled, infants and children, single mothers, the mentally ill, ex-prisoners, the homeless, the unemployed, the addicted, or those who lack healthcare. You can often develop a great social business idea by starting with the intended beneficiaries and then working backward.

The goal is to find a product or create a service that empowers your customers. Try to offer them something they do not just consume, but that gives them the chance to earn more or save more than they spend on your product. This could be credit with which your customers can set up their own businesses, increasing their income and giving them a chance to become financially independent. The product could also be related to education or information, which can enable customers to create more value through their economic activities. It could be related to healthcare, enabling them to work more productively. It could be access to electricity, machinery, or modern technology. Or it could be an insurance product to protect them from risks they cannot survive.

You do not need to think of a social business only in terms of selling a product. You can also think of a business that empowers people by helping them get better access to the markets of the developed world, or by giving them good jobs, or by giving them income through business ownership. In all these cases, your social business can enable less-fortunate people to capture a larger part of the value chain. If, for instance, you create a social business for textile products, you could sell the latest fashion at high prices to wealthy customers, but that would be just the means to an end. The real purpose could be to create good jobs for disadvantaged cotton farmers and textile workers. You would strive to maximize the number of people benefiting from the business operations and to maximize the individual benefit you could create for each of the workers.

Here are some other ideas you may find useful in triggering new social business concepts to serve a particular group of people you choose to target.

Improving production and access to markets. Do the people you want to serve currently work? Do they have valuable skills? Can you give them better access to attractive markets? Can you give them tools, training, or access to knowledge to increase the value they can create and the money they can make through their work? Your role could be on the production side or on the marketing side—for example, by finding a way to provide access to customers in the developed world for crafts workers or artisans from the developing world.

Providing employment. Your social business could be designed in such a way that you help people through giving them good jobs. You could set up a trading company and employ a sales force of former drug addicts or single mothers (where one parent might take care of the children while the other parents work). You could work with disabled people, designing a social business that uses their skills while making their disabilities irrelevant (for example, training sightless people to assemble furniture, sew garments, or even provide massages). You could create a collection of chain stores—fruit stands, pizzerias, newsstands, or what have you—and employ people to operate them. If convenient, you might eventually transfer ownership of these small businesses to the employees who run them, turning those individuals into micro-entrepreneurs in their own right.

Helping consumers. People can benefit from being able to purchase necessary and valuable products and services at affordable prices. This is what Grameen has done, from providing credit that helps people participate in local business markets and selling solar panels that provide a sustainable supply of electricity to marketing fortified yogurt that yields improved nutrition. Of course, one of the most potent products you can sell is education, from literacy training and basic vocational skills to language programs, computer courses, and technological training. You could also sell useful technology, such as access to Internet or mobile phone applications that help people to, for example, make better use of agricultural and other markets. To qualify as a social business, the products and services you sell should generate greater value for customers than they cost. They must also be affordable to those who need them most, whether by means of a moderate up-front cost, through generous credit terms that make long-term payment plans available, or through cross-subsidization by higher-priced sales to the more affluent.

Enabling entrepreneurship. One of the strongest lessons my life has taught me is that there is enormous creative and entrepreneurial potential in all people. Your social business could be set up in such a way as to encourage entrepreneurship. There are many ways to do this. You could create a center in which entrepreneurs are brought together with other people who have the knowledge, skills, experience, or technology needed to start successful businesses. You could set up an investment fund, a training program, or a marketing agency. You could create a mentorship program for aspiring entrepreneurs or sponsor contests to select, honor, and promote the best new business concepts. In time, you would be proud to point to a collection of thriving businesses that you helped to create.

Providing stability. One of the main problems poor people have is that their lives are not protected against economic, personal, and social shocks. Living at the edge of subsistence, it takes only a tiny blow to send them into a downward spiral that often ends in extreme poverty. The blow could be a single bad harvest, a serious accident or illness, an economic downturn, or a family crisis—a child suffering drug abuse, for instance. Perhaps you could create a social business that offers vulnerable people a greater degree of stability in their lives. You could think of ways to spread the risk across many people, much as an insurance company does. You could organize people into groups that support one another, as a cooperative does. There are probably even better ideas than this—perhaps you have the creativity to invent one.

Whatever need you seek to serve among the members of your target group, your social business will be much more effective if the people you hope to help are participating in its development. Make a connection with the people who will benefit from the business; invite them to be a part of the process. Don't forget that the poor and the disadvantaged are just as capable, entrepreneurial, and hardworking as you or anyone else. They are also just as talented at devising smart ideas for social business. After all, who understands the social needs of the poor better than the poor themselves? Creating such connections will not only yield a better business plan—it will also create an atmosphere of respect and greatly increase the chances that your social business will be successful.

Applying Technology to Human Needs

Another approach to developing a social business idea is to look at current or new technologies and to ask, "Is there a way this technology could serve human needs that is currently *not* being practiced?" Here are a few specific ideas along these lines that may trigger a eureka moment for you.

Increasing access to infrastructure. In many places where there is poverty, infrastructure is a problem. There may be a need for a bridge or a road to connect a village to a market. There may be no access to electricity or to clean water. The irrigation system for local farmers may be insufficient. There may be no recycling or other waste management, and there may be a high degree of pollution. Improving such infrastructure shortcomings may directly enable higher incomes. In many cases, the people affected may be willing to pay for the improvement of infrastructure.

A social business entrepreneur could pick one of these problems and start a modest-sized business to tackle it—the High Street Sewage Improvement Company, for example. After this project is successfully completed, you could move on to another project, and then another, and eventually launch bigger and bigger projects.

If you have access to the necessary resources, you could also tackle larger infrastructure issues: You could try to meet the need for a regional seaport to encourage commerce, for an airport to promote long-distance travel, or for power plants and transmission lines. Your role as the social business entrepreneur might be, among others, to organize such an undertaking, to find investors and technology, to organize a legal framework, to devise a revenue-gathering and-sharing model, or to find a way through regulatory and bureaucratic hurdles.

Adapting technologies used by the wealthy to the needs of the poor. Many of the technologies that have made life much better for the wealthy are now ready to be adapted, made more robust, and—above all—made cheaper so they can help the poor. The mobile phone is an obvious example. Back in 1997, when we set up a village phone network in Bangladesh and created a nationwide network of "telephone ladies," we simply took a new technology for the rich and made it available to the poor. Nowadays there are many other technologies that could be treated similarly: computing, the Internet, mobility, renewable energy, healthcare technologies, and so on. All that's needed is for social business entrepreneurs to come up with viable business models to bring these technologies within reach of everyone.

In some cases, off-the-shelf technology designed for the rich can be used by the poor without change. In other cases, there's a need for creative design to develop technologies that are just right for the poor. Some of the easy-to-use technologies produced for poor people may prove to be so powerful and attractive that the rich will rush to adopt them.

Enhancing sustainability and the environment through technological solutions. We can dramatically improve the natural environment through social businesses, producing benefits that will impact human health and economics in enormously positive ways. For example, if we can organize social businesses around such activities as forestation, watershed protection, fisheries management, eco-tourism, and sustainable farming, the long-term yield of agriculture will be higher and life in rural communities will be far more prosperous. The challenge for the social business entrepreneur will be to assemble the capital needed to make a transition to sustainable practices, to provide the knowledge and technology required, and to organize access to markets.

Testing the Model

Your goal as a social business entrepreneur is to create a business model that can be cost-effective while also providing a valuable service to the poor or to another underserved segment of society. This step usually calls for some creative thinking.

So take your time with brainstorming. Do a lot of research and reading. Examine ways that others have tried to solve the social problem, and try to pinpoint why they failed—and how they could have succeeded. And look at innovative solutions to different social problems and ask, "Is there any way this system could be changed and adapted to solve the problem I am studying?" Perhaps a clever concept from the field of transportation or information technology could be applied to healthcare, housing, or education—or vice versa.

Also spend time with the people you hope to serve. Get to know their interests, needs, abilities, and dreams. One of them may have the perfect solution in mind—if only someone like you would take the time to listen.

Once you have the idea for a business model, the next step is to test the idea. This experimental phase is crucial because it allows you to get a firm understanding of how feasible your idea is, what its strengths and weaknesses are, and what special skills, knowledge, and other resources you may need to put it into effect. The experimental phase will ultimately help you develop a working business model, and better understand how much money you will need in the future to set up a full-size operation.

As I've already emphasized, it is best to start small and start soon. As soon as your idea is formulated, begin asking yourself or the other members of your team: "How can we get a small pilot of our idea up and running? Are there organizations or community members we can reach out to immediately who will help us get started on a very small scale?"

Try to use minimal resources at this stage. Funding for your pilot project may have to come mainly from your own pocket. This is typical of many successful social entrepreneurs. I've already recounted how I got started in microlending with just $27 from my personal wallet. In a similar way, Dhruv Lakra in Mumbai, India, started testing his business idea for a courier service in 2008 with $300 saved up from his scholarship from Oxford University. He used the money to hire two hearing-impaired young men from local schools. Then he called some friends in his own personal network and asked them if they would like any packages delivered by his new courier service. A few people agreed to hire Lakra's tiny company. And with that he got his start in building a business that employs disabled people from impoverished backgrounds. Today, Mirakle Couriers employs thirty-five workers, all deaf, who deliver packages silently but with great efficiency throughout the city.

Would-be social entrepreneurs of today are especially fortunate. Thanks in part to modern technology, it's possible to experiment with a new business model on a shoestring budget. Do you really need to spend money on an office? Probably not—many businesses can be run out of a cell phone stuck in someone's pocket. Do you need to open a shop to sell products? Nowadays it is quick, easy, and cheap to set up an Internet storefront that can reach more customers than a high-street boutique. Do you need to hire a graphic artist and a printer to create informational brochures or advertisements for your social business?

You can probably create results that are close to professional level just by using a PC and a cheap printer—or recruit a friend from a local art college and outdo what even the professionals offer.

Of course, you can also save money during the experimental phase by starting your social business on a part-time basis. As the saying goes, "Don't quit your day job"—at least not until you know, through testing and experience, that your social business model will really work. For many entrepreneurs, the most exciting day in their lives is the one when they resign from their old careers and commit themselves fully to their new one.

Creatively Modifying an Existing Model

If you are interested in launching a social business, you don't necessarily have to devise an entirely new solution to the social problem you want to address. There are already many organizations that have developed creative and effective approaches to the worst problems our species faces. Start with research into and study of the history of attempts to address the problem you want to focus on. You may find an idea that inspires you and that you can replicate and adapt to a different environment.

If an existing social business has had success with the same problem you want to address—whether it's healthcare, education, pollution, or what have you—reach out to it. Share your ideas, ask questions, and learn as much as you can. Request a copy of the business plan—many organizations will be happy to share it with you. Perhaps there is even a "social franchising" option that will allow you to simply expand the reach of an existing social business. This process of imitation, replication, experimentation, and improvement is what enabled microcredit to grow from an obscure practice in the villages of Bangladesh into a worldwide movement that has improved the lives of at least 150 million families on five continents.

You can also learn from NGOs and traditional profit-maximizing businesses. Some non-profits have great income streams; in many cases, their models could be converted into social businesses. In the same way, there are great for-profit companies that do a fine job of working with disadvantaged groups, providing employment, or distributing products and services that make life better. You can copy their best practices, take away the element of personal profit, and thus make a social business.

Above all, don't be discouraged by a start that appears unpromising. When the first desktop computer came onto the market back in 1981, it had only 256 kB of memory—a tiny fraction of the memory found in even a cheap toy today. The first automobiles traveled at the shockingly high speed of five miles per hour. The Wright Brothers' first airplane flight lasted twelve seconds and covered all of 120 feet. This is how everything starts. Over time, many people—collaborators, rivals, imitators—add new features, devise clever improvements, and find ways to streamline and enhance the system. Each stage brings new excitement and opens new possibilities. Ideas keep stacking up to reach up to the sky.

Progress in social business will be like that. The amazing successes we celebrate today will appear crude and laughable ten, twenty, and fifty years from now—because those who come after us will have learned so much from our first, halting efforts.

And every step in the process has its value. Even the simple replication of an existing social business model has value, since it shows whether and how the model can be adapted to new circumstances—a different social setting, a different set of customers, a different economic system. And quite often a simple replication may turn into something much more. You may start by copying an existing social business, then one day say, "Hey, I have an idea for doing this better." Suddenly you find that you, too, are a social business pioneer. It's an exciting moment.

An Alternative Model:
The Social Business Owned by the Poor

Even profit-maximizing companies can be transformed into social businesses by giving full or majority ownership to the poor. This constitutes the Type II social business. Grameen Bank falls under this category, because it is owned by the poor people who are its borrowers. Every year dividends are paid to the bank's owners out of the profits generated through banking activity.

The poor could get the shares of these social businesses in the form of gifts by donors, or they could buy the shares with their own money. Grameen Bank borrowers buy their shares with their own money, through small automatic deductions from their accounts. These shares cannot be transferred to non-borrowers. Thus, the ownership of Grameen Bank will always remain with the poor people for whose benefit the bank was originally founded. The member/owners also vote annually to elect the bank's board of directors, which is made up of female borrowers. This board sets broad bank policies, while a committed professional team conducts the bank's day-to-day operations.

Bilateral and multilateral donors to developing nations could easily create Type II social businesses. For example, instead of having a multilateral or a bilateral donor give a developing country a loan or a grant to build a bridge, the donor could create a "bridge company" owned by a specifically-created trust whose mandate would be to make sure the bridge company operates in an efficient way and makes a profit. The trust would use the profit to improve the quality of life of the local poor by undertaking programs related to education, health, or income-building. Profits generated by the company could also be invested in building more bridges—or a combination of both. A committed management team could be given the responsibility of running the company. Many infrastructure projects—such as roads, highways, airports, seaports, and utility companies—could be built in this manner.

Existing conventional companies could also be converted into social businesses using this same model of ownership. For instance, a construction company could be established with the goal of creating employment, income, and economic growth in a stagnant town or village. Ownership of the company could be vested in a dedicated trust to benefit the disadvantaged families, or all families, living in the area. The trust could manage the company directly or through a management contract with another company. Unemployed local people could be hired as workers for the company, and the company would compete on an equal basis with profit-maximizing companies for any construction jobs that are available in the area. If well-managed, the social business would generate profits that could be used for the benefit of the local people, funding a new public school, a senior citizens' center, an upgraded water supply system, employment-generating social enterprises for the handicapped, and similar projects.

Soon we will see exactly how a social business of this kind would work. As I'll explain in a later chapter, we are already in the process of establishing this kind of social business as a joint venture between Grameen and the Otto trading company of Germany.

Otto Grameen Trust has already been created and the factory is under construction. We are also finalizing plans for another social business of this type with the giant Japanese clothing company, Uniqlo. We hope both of these companies will go into production by early 2011—and quickly begin delivering social benefits to the people of their communities.

Working with Partners

Most social businesses are likely to originate with one person, or perhaps with a small group of people—friends, work colleagues, or people with a shared interest in a particular social problem. Within such a small group, you may not have all the expertise, experience, ideas, and resources needed to make your social business idea into a reality. Don't let that stop you! Look around for others you can partner with.

This is a model that we at Grameen Bank have used repeatedly and with great success. As I've explained, a number of the early social businesses Grameen Bank has created have involved joint venture partners that are usually profit-driven entities—companies like Danone, Veolia Water, BASF, Intel, and adidas.

These joint ventures are true partnerships that draw upon the talent, expertise, and enthusiasm of both organizations. It's never the case that one party is actually running the show while the other party is simply "signing on" to gain public relations credit or enhanced prestige.

After the initial contact is made, and before the executives of our two organizations sit down to talk, we send over a general description of the concept so that the potential partner has no confusion or wrong ideas about social business. Often we invite the senior executives of partner companies to attend social business labs organized by Grameen Creative Labs in various cities in Asia and Europe. (I'll explain much more about the Grameen Creative Labs in a later chapter.) It's important for the partner companies to have a very clear idea about social business. Then we say, "If you are interested in exploring the possibility of a partnership with Grameen for this type of business, we'll be more than happy to talk to you."

If the potential partners are interested, we discuss a possible business concept jointly, generally based on some special area of expertise and experience that our partner has to offer. Sometimes they quickly get thrilled about the concept; sometimes they need to think more about it. It usually requires a few exploratory trips by their experts to Bangladesh before we finalize a working agreement, generally in the form of a nonbinding memorandum of understanding. The Yunus Centre in Dhaka organizes the discussions, facilitates visits and meetings, and arranges sessions on social businesses to clarify all the issues involved in social business. After going through the preliminary steps, both sides move toward developing a full business plan, drawing up legal articles of incorporation, and investing funds in the new business.

Our objective during this process is to move forward "with deliberate speed." It's important that both parties fully understand what they are promising before any public commitments are made. This is especially vital when dealing with a brand-new concept, such as social business. I want our partners, particularly when they come from the for-profit world, to be very clear about the fact that their sole reward from our joint venture will be the knowledge that they are doing something to help their fellow human beings. So far, I'm happy to say, the company executives I've dealt with have understood and supported this concept—even in cases where they felt they needed more time to commit their organizations to the creation of a social business.

At the same time, I believe in moving relatively quickly once a good idea is on the table. There's truth in the saying that "too much analysis sometimes leads to paralysis." When doing something new, I want to gather as much background information as possible—but once that is done, there's no substitute for plunging ahead with a first experiment or two. Happily, the top executives of our partner companies are generally eager to move fast, too. I've found that, in general, the problems that arise in the early months of a new social business are ones that no amount of prior study was likely to uncover. The only way to unearth such problems is to start the business and let them make themselves obvious. The sooner you get to work, the sooner you can begin making the necessary adjustments and improvements to your business model.

A partnership between an organization devoted to helping the poor and a corporation committed to maximizing profit is not a conventional one. Some people even see it as a bit of an "odd couple" pairing, involving partners with very different values and goals. As a result, people sometimes wonder whether there is genuine enthusiasm for social business on the part of the for-profit partners—or whether the joint venture is merely an empty gesture designed to enhance a company's image, meet demands for corporate social responsibility, and make a few executives feel good about themselves.

Journalists ask me this question a lot. One of the ways they frame it is by asking, "Is it possible that Danone is using you? Perhaps they are using the image of Muhammad Yunus and Grameen Bank to make their company appear as a friend of the world's poor people." The implication is that there is something dishonest about the support of Danone (or Veolia Water, or Otto, or BASF, or Intel . . .) for the concept of social business—and perhaps that I should be resentful of this attempt to "use" my good name and that of Grameen Bank to enhance a corporation's prestige.

I avoid getting into debates over this issue. It's certainly possible to interpret the behavior of our corporate partners in many ways. Can anyone determine exactly how excited the Danone executives were to participate with us in a joint venture? Were they motivated by social intentions, by the desire to burnish their corporate reputation, by a personal belief in corporate responsibility, by the public's desire for a business role model to admire, by their pride in their company . . . or perhaps by some complicated combination of all these motives? No one can say. And frankly these questions were not running through my mind when I first met Franck Riboud, the CEO of Danone. He appeared genuinely interested in my proposal for a social business to help the children of Bangladesh. That was an exciting thing for me—and everything else is of secondary importance.

So my response when reporters ask me whether Danone is "using" me is to reply, "Is that so? I thought I was using Danone! Because the involvement of such a big company immediately transforms social business from an unimportant notion into a legitimate concept that every businessperson in Europe wants to know about. So I think I am using Danone to promote my idea. But if you are right—if Danone is actually using me—you can tell the world that I am here to be used.

Please use me! Anybody who wants to use me is most welcome to do that—for a good cause."

And social business is that cause.

Of course, the Grameen Danone and Grameen Veolia Water joint ventures gain enormously from the resources of the big companies that are behind them, especially the business expertise they bring to the table. But another important benefit that grows out of such joint ventures is the effect they have on our corporate partners and, through them, on the business world as a whole.

This impact is seen, in part, in how working on social business has affected the employees of Danone and Veolia Water. The executives from those companies report that their colleagues are deeply excited by the fact that their organizations are involved in this new experiment in progressive business. People stop them in the hall to ask how the Grameen joint venture is doing, to offer support, to volunteer to join the project, to ask when the next social business will be launched. Social business is one of the topics that workers from Danone and Veolia Water tend to brag about when they talk about their jobs to outsiders; it's something that new graduates ask about when they apply for positions at those firms. BASF's CEO, Dr. Jürgen Hambrecht, even required his company's 245 top managers from around the world to read my book before they assembled for their annual headquarters conference in September 2008. Then he invited me to address the conference and answer their questions.

This personal effect seems likely to outlast the specific social businesses that gave rise to it. Suppose Veolia Water were to announce, "We are too busy to continue work on the Grameen Veolia Water business." What would happen? First, the drinking-water initiative itself would continue, because we've learned a lot about how to do it from our work with Veolia Water. Furthermore, I would wager that some of the people Grameen has worked with at Veolia Water would volunteer to continue providing us with ideas and help, even without being financially supported by the company. And the same is true of Danone.

Veolia Water and Danone are companies, but they are made up of people. Not only are we changing things in the business world, but we are also changing the people inside the business.

I don't mean to imply that Veolia Water and Danone are going to be transformed into social businesses. We are building a parallel path in collaboration with the for-profit company—a path for social business. This path will gain its own momentum. And the experience of people within our joint venture partners will help to build that momentum. One day, some of them may retire from their for-profit careers and launch social business ventures of their own. And others who remain within Veolia Water and Danone (and the other companies we are partnering with) will increasingly apply the values and creative thinking that shape social business in their daily for-profit jobs. They will ask new questions: "What are we doing to make our new products available to poor people?" "How can we make our business more socially and environmentally sustainable?" "What benefits will our new factory bring to the people of the neighboring community?" Little by little, traditional business may begin to reflect the influence of social business.

I don't see Groupe Danone becoming a social business, but I would not be surprised if someday there is a new company—perhaps called Danone Social—that is dedicated entirely to social business. That's the kind of long-term impact I believe our partnerships with companies may have.

So even aside from the practical value that a partnership can have when launching a social business, there are far-reaching benefits to be created by involving other organizations in developing the social business concept.

Here are some examples of the kinds of organizations you may want to consider partnering with when launching your own social business:

- *Another social business*—to replicate, adapt, or expand an existing model
- *An NGO or charity*—to complement and support the existing work of an NGO with your new social business
- *An investor*—a private individual, a company, an investment fund, a philanthropic foundation, or even a governmental body that is looking for a way to create a positive social effect with its investment monies
- *A technology partner*—to sell or license the technological products or expertise needed to make your social business successful, or to join the project as a partner, providing the technology as its contribution
- *A production partner*—to provide you with either raw materials for your own production or final products for you to sell
- *A human resources partner*—for example, an agency that might connect you with talented people who are willing to dedicate part of their careers to a worthwhile cause, or a university that might link you to professors or students with relevant expertise
- *A distribution partner*—which could be an NGO (if you want to sell a product to poor customers), a traditional profit-maximizing business (if you want to sell a product to wealthy customers), or an Internet marketer (if you want to sell a product to customers who are technologically savvy and widely dispersed geographically)
- *A monitoring partner*—an organization that can help you define and measure the effect of your social business, which could be a non-profit organization, a think tank, or a university team with expertise in the area you'll be working on. The better your monitoring, the easier it will be to convince investors and other partners of the value of your work

Of course, you might find yourself working with several of these kinds of partners as your needs, capabilities, and circumstances change.

The ability to forge and maintain positive, creative relationships with partner organizations is likely to be one of the hallmarks of the most successful social businesses.

Attracting Talent

Even the smallest social business will need to take on employees. It will need to hire more and more people as it grows. Which leads to the question: Does a social business relate to human talent in a different way than does a profit-maximizing business?

It seems to me that the answer to this question depends on the answer to an even deeper question: Is the desire to impact the world as strong as the desire to make money? That's the whole issue.

Often I argue that making an impact on people's lives is every bit as inspiring and fulfilling as making money—or even more so. Try it. You may get mesmerized by your capacity to change the world for the better. You'll want to do it more and faster. You'll find yourself lying awake at night, dreaming about the amazing things you want to try as soon as you get to work the next morning. The social business entrepreneur is often just as obsessed with success as the profit-driven entrepreneur. The only difference lies in how "success" is defined.

Many people assume that employees of a social business don't get paid well—that nobody should expect a good salary from a social business. After all, the idea of social business is to help people. So the key to attracting employees must be to appeal to "do-gooders" who are willing to sacrifice their own interests for the benefit of society.

That's a very wrong idea about social business. Social business pays you *more*, not less.

First, a social business has to attract talent from the same labor market that for-profit companies plumb. That means offering competitive salaries and benefits. If you want a good accountant, a good marketing manager, or a good production expert for your social business, you'll have to offer the same kind of compensation package that a bank, automaker, or computer company would offer.

Once this basic requirement is met, the personal rewards offered by a social business employer are actually *greater* than those offered by traditional businesses.

Suppose an accountant has two job offers in hand, one from a profit-making company, one from a social business. Both offer the same salary, similar benefits, and comparable job titles and responsibilities.

It seems to me that most people will weigh the two offers this way: "What's the difference between these two jobs? The main difference is that the social business offers me the opportunity to change the world—to become part of the solution rather than part of the problem. I'll come home from work every day with the satisfaction of knowing that I am engaged in solving a problem that otherwise would have remained unsolved. I'll feel good knowing that I am making a difference. If the financial rewards are equal, why not take the social business job?"

I write about this issue from the practical perspective of a businessperson who has actually founded, grown, and run social businesses. Grameen Bank and the other social businesses I am involved with have long faced the challenge of hiring and retaining smart, hardworking, and talented employees in competition with leading companies. I am happy to say that we have had no difficulty attracting first-rate people. As with any company, some stay with us for just a short time—two or three years, perhaps. But most of them work with us for their entire careers.

Several of the top officials of Grameen Bank began working with me as graduate students in my economics courses at Chittagong University, when lending to the poor was just a funny idea we were experimenting with. Almost thirty years later they are still members of my team. And like anyone else they have raised families, sent children to college, owned homes, and saved money for retirement. Working for a social business doesn't require sainthood or self-sacrifice. It just means caring about making the world a better place—and I think this motivation exists inside practically every person on Earth.

Planning Your Social Business

In many ways, a social business is like any other business. It has employees and managers, customers and suppliers. It offers goods or services at a price that it hopes the marketplace will find attractive. It has expenses to cover, payrolls to meet, and rents to pay. All these financial parameters must be spelled out accurately and thoughtfully in a realistic, practical business plan.

So planning a social business is in many ways similar to planning a profit-maximizing business. Before launching the business, you will want to create a business plan that outlines your objectives and the means you will use to pursue them. For a small, simple social business, the business plan may be very basic—just a few pages of notes and numbers spelling out your program. For a more complicated business, a longer, more detailed, more complex plan may be required. If you hope to get financing from a bank or an outside investor, a detailed business plan will probably be necessary.

It's not my intention to teach you all the details about how to create a business plan. And in any case, I don't think that extensive knowledge of business is a crucial requirement for someone who wants to start a social business.

You don't need to know "how to do business." Much more important is your desire to solve a social problem. To be sure, practical knowledge about doing business will be useful. If you do not have experience, you will learn as you go along—hopefully with a mentor, an investor, or a partner to challenge and support you. But established business knowledge may be counterproductive in the context of social business. It may lead you to think in the wrong directions—how to reduce costs and optimize operations irrespective of the social benefit of the processes; how to skillfully advertise a product that may not be of great benefit to the consumer; how to undermine your competitors; and so on. In a social business, the aim is not to maximize profit, crush rivals, or grow for the sake of growth. The aim is to deliver a social benefit, with smart financial and managerial policies as a means to that end. For that reason, the right motivation and the dedication to carry the business through are more important than having the right business tools.

Nonetheless, a business plan is very important. It may be revised as you go along, but don't start without one. If you're a business novice, I recommend replicating an existing model as your first step in the world of social business. Copying someone else's business plan that has already been proven successful will be a relatively easy undertaking—don't feel compelled to reinvent the wheel in your first venture.

Whether it is a new creation or a replication of someone else's model, your business plan should address all the same basic issues as in any business plan:

- What product or service will I offer?
- How will I produce this product or service?
- Who are my customers?
- How many are there?
- How do they make their buying decisions?
- How can I find out what price they are willing to pay for the product or service I will offer?
- What is my competition?
- What methods of marketing, distributing, advertising, selling, and promoting my product or service will I use?
- What are the initial capital expenses I must meet in order to launch the business?
- What are the monthly expenses I can expect (rent, payroll, employee benefits, utilities, supplies, transportation, and so on)?
- How will my expenses change as my volume of business grows?

- What revenue from sales can I realistically expect during my first month in business? My first six months? My first year? My first three years?
- Based on the figures presented above, when can I expect to reach the break-even point?
- Over what time period can I expect to repay the initial capital (in the form of investment funds or loans) used to launch the business?

All these questions are the same ones that any business plan should answer. But because you are launching a social business, you'll also need to address some additional questions, including:

- What is my social objective: Whom do I expect to help with my social business?
- What social benefits do I intend to provide?
- How will the intended beneficiaries of my business participate in planning and shaping the business?
- How will the impact of my social business be measured?
- What social goals do I hope to achieve in my first six months? In my first year? In my first three years?
- If my social business is successful, how can it be replicated or expanded?
- Are there additional social benefits that can be added to the package of offerings I will create?

As these additional questions suggest, a social business must be *better run* than a conventional for-profit company. After all, the objectives to be pursued are more complex and demanding—and, I would argue, they are also more important.

There are some other crucial differences between a conventional business plan and the business plan a social business requires.

One difference is that the plan for a social business must be *responsible*. A social business should be committed to pursuing its social goals without harming anyone, while minimizing its impact on the environment.

We've applied this principle to the Grameen Danone joint venture. Our yogurt plant in Bogra has recycling facilities, solar power cells, and other "green" features. I also insisted that the yogurt container be biodegradable—no plastic is allowed. The experts at Danone wrestled with that requirement for a while and finally found a supplier in China that manufactured a cup made of cornstarch that was completely biodegradable.

I was pleased, but not fully satisfied. I looked at this cornstarch cup and asked, "Could I eat it? Why should poor people pay for this container that has to be thrown away? Why can't you make an edible cup? Children will eat the cup after they finish the yogurt, and that way they will receive even more nutrition." The Danone research team in Paris is working on meeting this goal. I predict they'll do it—and that the result may someday revolutionize food packaging.

Of course, all businesses have certain minimal social responsibilities they must meet. There are laws and regulations that every company must follow, as well as ethical standards (such as honesty) that every businessperson should live up to. Ultimately, however, the responsibility that comes with a social business is much higher than with a traditional business. It is even more important to understand your customers and their needs. After all, the aim of social business is to solve a problem: poverty, malnutrition, disease, ignorance, homelessness. It may not solve the whole problem, but it should move the world in the right direction. And it certainly should not *create* new problems through its business methods. So for a social business to exploit workers, pollute the environment, or sell defective and dangerous products would be even worse than for a conventional business to commit these sins.

At the same time, creating a social business that is sustainable over time is very necessary. Your goal is to provide people with lasting benefits. If the business is sustainable only under certain conditions, or for a limited period of time, you'll have to look for more robust solutions. Social businesses can fail, like conventional businesses. But a social business has a special responsibility. Once a community comes to depend on your social business, you don't want to let its members down. So bring to your social business all the intelligence, management savvy, dedication, compassion, and hard work that you would bring to any fledgling company—and then some.

A Journey of a Thousand Miles

I generally urge people who are setting up a social business to start small. A simple business is easier to run, and a pilot project will yield insights and experience that can help you refine and improve your business plan. But even more important is to start at all. Your first days and weeks working in social business will open your eyes to new possibilities. They will give you a first glimpse of the joy you feel when you help people—even just a single person.

You probably know the old saying, "A journey of a thousand miles begins with a single step." Take the first step! Don't worry too much about the miles to come—they will take care of themselves, as long as you keep putting one foot in front of the other.

Try to find a model that works. It may take a lot of experimentation. You will twist and tweak your business model until you are satisfied that you are addressing the social problem in a manner that is empowering and economically sustainable. You can easily change things as necessary or even scrap the idea entirely and start from scratch. Do not become overly frustrated. Remember, social business is still a very new idea. You are an innovator, a pioneer. You are doing very demanding work and may find yourself in a place where no one has been before. There is no straight path to success. Be persistent and patient, and do not lose your enthusiasm. The process of finding a model that works may take years. There is always a learning curve to be negotiated.

But it is worth it. If you develop a great model, you will find plenty of potential customers to grow it and plenty of other entrepreneurs who want to copy and implement it elsewhere. You and your followers can scale your operations rapidly and have a vast impact. You will not only change many people's lives, but you may also change the very fabric of our social and economic systems. You will join many others who are doing the same. And together we will reach the large goals we have set for ourselves: to end poverty, to create a sustainable way of living, to empower the disenfranchised, to extinguish diseases. I really see no limit to the possibilities—provided we have the courage to take the first step.

CHAPTER 4

To Cure One Child

A Case of Social Business in Healthcare

Most of us are very impatient by nature. We want to fix things quickly. It's especially true with the huge, global problems that have burdened humankind for centuries: poverty, disease, hunger, homelessness, oppression. Those of us who worry about such things sometimes count up the terrible numbers—the billions of poor people, the hundreds of millions who are hungry or thirsty or ill—and we want to create a plan that will solve the problem overnight. After all, these problems have been with us far too long already. Why should we put up with them even a single day longer?

This attitude is understandable, even praiseworthy. But for practical reasons it is sometimes better to reduce a problem to a manageable size rather than trying to fix it all at once. Giant plans designed to help millions of people at once often get out of control. Unless we prepare step by step, "thinking big" can be a recipe for disaster.

When I speak with young people about social business, I don't try to change their impatience. We *should* be impatient with the terrible social problems we have created and imposed on our fellow humans. But I suggest a different *kind* of impatience. Instead of trying to devise giant plans to change the world all at once, I urge them to "start small." Create a tiny plan to help a few people at a time—and rather than spending months or years refining, developing, and funding it, put it into practice *immediately*, and learn as you proceed to implement. In a small project, you can see that some parts of your plan are working beautifully, while other parts do not work at all, and still other parts look weak. You may even find that something is happening in your project that you never dreamed about. Then you can use all your experience to improve your plan.

In time you will have a social business that is brilliantly effective at making life better for a few people. It is a seed that can then be replicated once, twice, ten times, a hundred times, a thousand times. Success in achieving big goals lies in designing one small basic module, a multiple of which makes up the big plan. Developing such a seed is critical in solving mega-problems.

Once you have developed the seed, the next important thing to do is to design a management structure for multiplication of the seed with a smooth exponential growth path. Who knows? One day it may end up being the germ of a global change that solves a worldwide problem for hundreds of millions of people.

One of the benefits of this kind of impatience is that it allows anybody and everybody to get involved in social business. You may be a student, a homemaker, a young business executive, an active or retired CEO, a jobless person, a retiree, an academic, a worker, or whatever. No matter your background, you can express your creativity by designing a tiny social business plan and implementing it with support from a few other people.

The examples presented in this book may create the impression that a social business can be launched only through a partnership with a big corporation with lots of experience, money, and other resources—companies like Danone, Veolia Water, BASF, Otto, Intel, adidas, and others. These examples show that even hard-nosed, giant global companies are finding social business an attractive idea. But the real power of social business is in the opportunities it creates for a single person, or a small group of friends, with much more modest resources, operating on a very small scale, to create a business that can someday have a global effect.

And it's impossible to predict which starting point will prove, in the end, to produce the greatest impact. Remember, I started Grameen Bank not with a business plan for serving millions of people, but by lending the equivalent of $27 to forty-two people in the village of Jobra. So start small—and start *today*. Learn as you go, and don't give until you've found the right design.

In this chapter, I'll describe the example of a modest-scale social business being developed by two inspired, caring young men from Italy—a physician named Lawrence Faulkner and an entrepreneur named Eugenio La Mesa. Together with a handful of friends and supporters, they have embarked on a journey to address one of the world's most devastating genetic diseases, thalassemia, by creating an NGO called Cure2Children. A joint venture social business will start functioning by the second half of 2010, based on a partnership between this NGO and Grameen Healthcare Trust.

Their journey began by providing a cure for a handful of children who otherwise would be doomed to a very short and painful life. The satisfaction was immediate—and the long-term potential is enormous.

You may be unfamiliar with the disease known as thalassemia. It is a terrible genetic disorder that affects the blood of children who are unlucky enough to suffer from it. Like sickle cell anemia, thalassemia is carried by a recessive gene. A person with a single gene for thalassemia suffers no symptoms and is often unaware that he or she is a carrier. But if the mother and father are both carriers, each child has a one-in-four chance of inheriting two thalassemia genes. Such a child begins to suffer from anemia within a few months of birth. Survival depends on repeated blood transfusions. And even with this treatment, few thalassemia victims in poor countries survive much beyond eighteen years of age.

Because it is transmitted genetically, thalassemia is most common among certain population groups. At one time, it was rampant around the Mediterranean—Italy, Greece, Spain. Today, however, thalassemia has almost disappeared in Europe and elsewhere in the wealthy nations of the world, thanks to genetic screening. Because the disease can be detected through a simple blood test, every pregnant woman in both Europe and the United States is screened for thalassemia. If her unborn child exhibits the condition, she can choose a therapeutic abortion. Even earlier, couples who are planning to get married are routinely tested for the thalassemia gene. Those who test positive are encouraged not to produce any offspring. Instead, these couples are encouraged to adopt children.

Now that genetic screening has virtually eliminated thalassemia in Europe and America, the disease is found primarily in some countries of the developing world—in particular in South Asia, where a significant fraction of the population carries the telltale gene. In some parts of South Asia, frequent intermarriage makes the problem worse. In families where thalassemia is widespread, it greatly increases the odds that a mother and father will share the gene and pass it along to their offspring.

In Bangladesh today, an estimated 100,000 children are suffering from thalassemia, and between 6,000 and 7,000 new cases arise every year. Of course, thalassemia is just one of many afflictions that strike children in Bangladesh in excessive numbers. But for every family that has a child with this condition, it is an unspeakable tragedy.

It is also a problem that is within reach of being solved through genetic screening. Such a program has been shown to work in Europe and North America, and there is no reason to doubt it could work in the rest of the world, including South Asia. The only obstacles are poverty, lack of access to medical care and counseling, and simple lack of awareness. All of these barriers can be surmounted through determined effort.

At the same time, we need to provide a cure for individuals already suffering from thalassemia—an actual cure that goes beyond palliative care in the form of blood transfusions. While such cures are being developed through experimentation in several parts of the world, a brilliant Italian doctor, Dr. Guido Lucarelli, had success in devising a cure around 1984.

Using adult stem cells from a specially matched donor, Dr. Lucarelli found that he could perform a complete bone marrow transplant for certain patients suffering from thalassemia. The operation is time-consuming, difficult, extensive, and physically traumatic; afterward, the patient must remain in the hospital for an average of forty-five days, recovering from the process. However, when it is performed in a low-risk, otherwise healthy patient with a compatible sibling, the operation generally yields a complete cure for thalassemia. No more blood transfusions are required, the patient can live a normal life, and the death sentence is lifted. It's truly a medical miracle.

Dr. Lawrence Faulkner learned this new transplant method directly from Dr. Lucarelli. Born in Florence, Italy, Dr. Faulkner received his training at the University of Florence, at Long Island College Hospital in Brooklyn, New York, and at Memorial Sloan-Kettering Cancer Center in New York City. Then he returned to Italy, where he helped to create one of the world's leading centers for performing transplantations and training other doctors in the techniques. In addition to thalassemia patients, he also cared for patients with a variety of other illnesses, especially leukemia and other forms of blood-related cancer.

It was a tragedy that struck two of his patients that led Dr. Faulkner to wonder whether he could take on the menace of thalassemia in the developing world.

Two small children both died of a rare cancer called neuroblastoma, despite months of treatment by Dr. Faulkner and his colleagues. As you can imagine, the parents were heartbroken. But they were also determined to make something good emerge from their heartbreak. They visited Dr. Faulkner, to whom they had become quite close during the months of trying to save their children's lives, and they told him, "Dr. Faulkner, we'd like to do something to spare other families what we've been through. Do you have any ideas?"

He did. "You could start a foundation to help other families here in Italy," he said. "But I want to make a different suggestion. Why not start an organization that will provide medical care to poor children with rare blood diseases in the poorest countries of the world?"

Dr. Faulkner's suggestion was not based simply on altruism. In fact, there was an important scientific motive behind it. There are thousands of sick kids in the developing world who don't have access to medical care. Many of the rare cancers and blood disorders that take their lives go untreated and also unstudied, since these cases may occur anywhere—in a remote village in India, in a city slum in Bangladesh, in the jungle in Africa. And these cases, while tragic to the families involved, are potentially precious to physicians and scientists.

"Take neuroblastoma as an example," Dr. Faulkner explained to the families. "This condition is very rare in Italy. We know of just fifty patients per year in this country. This makes it very difficult to build up a knowledge base for improving treatment.

"Yet thousands of cases of neuroblastoma are believed to occur in the countries of the developing world, scattered in hundreds of locations and tracked, if at all, by doctors in hundreds of local hospitals, with no way to compare their experiences and learn from them.

"If we could begin to extend medical care to poor people in the developing world, it could create a win-win situation. We could bring help, including cures, to those suffering from disease, and at the same time we could gather a wealth of knowledge about the rare ailments that today are considered mysterious."

The parents who had approached Dr. Faulkner understood this message and quickly agreed to support the idea. Additional funding was provided by a foundation associated with a large Italian bank. Dr. Faulkner arranged to take a one-year sabbatical from his regular work assignments in Florence. In January 2007 he began working to create what became known as Cure2Children—a non-profit organization dedicated to researching, developing, and providing treatments for rare cancers and blood diseases to the children of the world.

Another personal connection played a role in shaping Dr. Faulkner's specific mission. In the Children's Hospital in Florence, he often cared for children from around the world whose parents had brought them there to work with the advanced specialists. One of these children was a baby girl from Pakistan who was suffering from thalassemia. In collaboration with a colleague, Dr. Pietro Sodani, Dr. Faulkner performed transplantation on this baby girl using a risky, innovative procedure in which the mother, rather than a sibling, serves as the donor. (In this case, there was no sibling with the required matching characteristics.)*

The difficult operation was a complete success: The baby girl's life was saved, and in the process, the two doctors formed a strong personal bond with her parents. It so happened that the baby's mother was herself a physician. When Dr. Faulkner told these parents about his plan to bring world-class treatments for rare blood disorders to the developing world, they immediately agreed that Pakistan would be an ideal place to begin the project, and that thalassemia could be the chief target for their work. The little girl's mother, Dr. Sadaf Khalid, is now the director of the Pakistan branch of Cure2Children; the father works in the Ministry of the Interior in Pakistan.

It was quite a bold move for Dr. Faulkner to undertake this project in Pakistan. While he had developed a fine level of cross-cultural sensitivity when caring for the patients from Asia and elsewhere during his work in the children's hospital in Florence, he had never actually worked in a developing country. But his training in the United States combined with his work in Florence, creating a world-class transplant service and laboratory from the ground up, had given him valuable

---

*Sodani, Faulkner, and other physicians and researchers in Florence have continued to develop this new procedure, and in 2010 they published a groundbreaking paper on the topic in *Blood,* the medical journal published by the American Society of Hematology.

insights into the strengths and weaknesses of differing kinds of health-care systems—high-tech America versus "high-touch" Italy; privately run America versus state-run Italy. With the help of his two doctor partners from Pakistan, he felt ready to make the move.

Today, Cure2Children is curing thalassemia in Pakistan. Using donor funding, it established a two-bed unit dedicated to bone marrow transplantation at the Children's Hospital of the Pakistan Institute of Medical Sciences in Islamabad. Start-up costs were a very modest 25,000 euros (about $35,000). Continuing expenses are also quite small. The fifteen people the facility employs, ranging from nurses to technical specialists, earn a *total* monthly salary of around 4,000 euros (roughly $5,600). So lives are being saved for an amazingly small price.

At the moment, the effort is on a small scale, especially when compared with the many potential patients (estimated at 50,000 in Pakistan). As of December 2009, Dr. Faulkner and his team had performed twenty transplant operations, with outcomes comparable to those obtained in Italy. In time, more such units will be opened in other hospitals around the country. Eventually, life-saving operations should become available to all the children in Pakistan who need them.

To be clear, Cure2Children's programs in Pakistan and Kosovo are *not* run according to the social business model. Cure2Children is a traditional NGO that relies on charitable giving.

Now, Cure2Children is preparing to bring its life-saving techniques and technologies to Bangladesh in collaboration with Grameen Healthcare Trust, within the framework of a social business.

The idea of using the social business model came into focus when the CEO of Cure2Children, an energetic and persuasive young man named Eugenio La Mesa, read *Creating a World Without Poverty*. Fascinated by the new idea of social business, he sent me an e-mail describing his organization's work in Pakistan and soliciting my collaboration in bringing it to Bangladesh as a social business. In this e-mail, La Mesa wrote, in part:

Cure2Children is not a social business, because it gets money from donors in Italy and spends it in developing countries to cure poor children who have severe diseases (mainly thalassemia). . . . But I'm extremely fascinated with your idea of a social business and I'm starting to think what I could do, especially in healthcare in developing countries, that is something that interests me a lot. . . . If you or one of your colleagues have an idea of how Cure2Children could become a social business, please let me know; in the meanwhile, I'll keep thinking and brainstorming about it.

I quickly replied with an e-mail of my own:

I am delighted to hear from you. We are taking a big initiative in Bangladesh to design and deliver healthcare as a social business. Your proposal to launch an initiative in curing thalassemia in Bangladesh will fit perfectly. We would like to have more discussion about it.

A series of e-mails, conversations, and meetings between his organization and my Grameen team followed. Today we are on the way to launching a social business for treating thalassemia in Bangladesh under a joint venture between Cure2Children and Grameen Healthcare Trust.

But how can bone marrow transplantation be made into a self-supporting business—especially in a country with a lot of poor people? Here is where creativity and careful planning are necessary.

The key to making this service economically self-sufficient will be cross-subsidization. Well-off families that can afford to pay the standard rate for bone marrow transplant operations will help to pay for poor families that can contribute little or nothing.

According to the current business plan, crafted by Eugenio La Mesa and the Grameen team led by Imamus Sultan, Cure2Children will begin by creating two transplant units in two selected hospitals in Bangladesh, each consisting of three patient beds. Two of these beds will be available to full price patients, while the third will serve a poor child whose parents will pay a token fee or none. When the resulting revenues and expenses are calculated, the unit should be self-supporting.

Each of these units should be able to perform between seven and ten operations per year. Over time, more units will be established in Bangladesh. At the same time, once the social business program has been tested and refined, the joint venture company will begin planning its next big leap—to implement the same system on an even larger scale in India. Each element of this plan reflects extremely careful planning and thought.

For example, there is the element of cost. The joint venture company expects to charge its well-off patients the equivalent of $20,000 for each bone marrow transplantation. This should be sufficient to cover the expenses of the unit, including doctors' fees, salaries for five nurses and other support personnel, equipment maintenance, and so on. Twenty thousand dollars is a lot of money. But it is just one-tenth the usual cost of a bone marrow transplant in the United States or Europe.

How will it be possible to locate a sufficient number of affluent families to occupy those two full-price beds and thereby subsidize the care of a poor child? The answer involves several pieces.

First, there should not be a problem in finding eight to twelve paying patients per year for the first two units. There are many families who are paying the monthly cost of blood transfusions today in Bangladesh, and this amount is not beyond their capacity. Second, when more units are added, the joint venture can treat patients from neighboring countries, too. Furthermore, patients may come from other Asian and African countries when these units build up their reputation.

The appeal of these transplantation units in Bangladesh should be quite strong. If you come from a well-off family in Asia or Africa and have a child in desperate need of a life-saving operation, one option might be to travel to Rome, London, or New York—and spend anywhere from $200,000 to $400,000, once expenses for travel and family accommodations are taken into account. (Remember, a child recovering from a bone marrow transplant must stay in the hospital for forty-five days. Think how much it costs for a family to stay in a hotel near the hospital for forty-five days!)

An attractive alternative would be to travel instead to a country like Bangladesh, where the culture is familiar and where the expense would be only one-tenth as great. There are many more people who could afford this than could afford to go to Italy, for example.

Add in another important fact—that the same bone marrow transplantation technology can be used in treating a number of conditions other than thalassemia, including leukemia, lymphoma, multiple myeloma, and sickle cell anemia. This also increases the number of patients for whom treatment in Bangladesh might well be a viable option.

Of course, to attract patients from other countries, the quality of the service provided must be just as high as that found in Italy or the United States. No one wants to compromise on healthcare for a sick child, even to save money. With support from Cure2Children, it appears that this objective can be reached.

High-tech communications and information technology will be one factor making this possible. You recall that one of the main reasons Dr. Faulkner was eager to begin serving patients in the developing world was to establish a large patient base for learning about rare blood diseases and cancers. With this goal in mind, Cure2Children has placed a lot of emphasis on creating a world-class IT and communications system to connect its professionals around the world.

Cure2Children wants to be a learning organization, and so it has created an open-source Web platform specially designed to allow easy, continuous communication among its professional teams in Italy, Pakistan, and soon in Bangladesh. Skype and Yugma—two Internet-based telecommunications tools—make it easy to conduct presentations and seminars from remote locations. Other software tools are used to facilitate project management and information-sharing by all members of the organization. As a result, it is now easy for world-class medical experts based in Florence, Rome, or Milan to consult with physicians and nurses in Islamabad or Dhaka about their patients on a daily basis.

Early in this chapter, I referred to a small-scale social business as a seed that can have an enormous impact over time. One reason I am excited about the joint venture between Cure2Children and Grameen Healthcare Trust is that it has so much potential to help improve healthcare in Bangladesh.

One element in this potential is the design of the joint venture company as a learning organization, focused as much on developing and spreading expertise as on providing care to particular patients. All the transplants performed in Bangladesh will be done by local doctors, not by experts who "parachute in" from Europe or America. This is the same model that Cure2Children has already used successfully in Pakistan. In Islamabad, Drs. Faulkner and Sodani trained two doctors in the same transplant techniques they learned from Dr. Lucarelli, while a separate team of experts from Italy trained a group of local nurses. The Italians remained in Pakistan for a month to observe and coach the first operations and confirmed that the expertise transfer had been successful.

The sharing of knowledge continues to this day. Cure2Children uses special software to allow the Pakistani nurses to share patient information with the team members in Italy on a daily basis. As needed, Dr. Faulkner and his Italian colleagues schedule conference calls with their counterparts in Pakistan to discuss tricky or complicated cases. "In the past," Dr. Faulkner explains, "we used to train individual physicians from the developing world at our center in Italy, one doctor at a time. This system is much more powerful. It enables us to create an entire team of skilled professionals who can then spread their knowledge to others in the community."

Dr. Faulkner has found the experience of training doctors and nurses in South Asia to be very rewarding. They are very motivated and recognize that the chance to study under a world-renowned expert in transplantation represents a great opportunity for them.

Do cultural differences pose any challenges when an Italian trains professionals from an Asian country? Dr. Faulkner smiles. "Sometimes Asian males have the same trait as men from other countries—it is hard for them to say things like, 'I don't understand,' or 'I made a mistake.' This is easier for women. So we have had great success in training female physicians in Pakistan. Perhaps the same will be true in Bangladesh."

Most important, bringing the advanced technology of bone marrow transplantation to Bangladesh will represent an important step forward for our entire healthcare system. Dr. Faulkner reports that in Cure2Children's Pakistani program, not a single nurse has left her job so far (in a profession where turnover is usually rather high). The good salary is one reason. But a more important one is that they are challenged, interested, and motivated by the high level of care they are able to provide. We have the same goal for Bangladesh.

Here is an example of the power of social business. I began my professional life as a teacher of economics; Dr. Faulkner began his as a medical practitioner focused on childhood cancers. Yet here we are, years later, converging on the same underlying issue: *How can vital goods (financial services, healthcare) be made available at the same level of quality for poor people in the developing world as for wealthy people in the developed nations?* And both of us have become convinced that social business provides the answer. The details differ from banking to medicine, but many of the underlying principles are the same.

In the long run, the goal for both Cure2Children and the joint venture with Grameen Healthcare Trust is to wipe out thalassemia altogether—in Bangladesh and in the world. Achieving this will depend on prevention—and this is a matter of education, communication, and prenatal screening and counseling for families throughout the society. It will take time—perhaps fifteen to twenty years—but it is very achievable.

Fortunately, information about thalassemia—what causes it, how it is transmitted—is becoming more widespread. In Italy, Dr. Lucarelli, the creator of the transplant cure, hears from patients all around the world who learn about him and his work through a network of associations of the families of thalassemia patients. Such associations exist in South Asia—for example, the thalassemia association in Chittagong, the second-largest city in Bangladesh, has 5,000 members. There are thalassemia associations in other parts of the country as well. These associations provide a good base from which to expand education about the importance of prevention.

The transplant centers that our joint venture will establish can also play a crucial role. Not every child who suffers from thalassemia is a candidate for a transplant operation. Low-risk patients have a 90 percent chance of a successful operation and an expected high quality of life; for high-risk patients, the success rate is closer to 50 percent, and the expected quality of life is lower. If Bangladesh has some 100,000 thalassemia cases, I am told that 30 percent would qualify as low-risk. These are the ones to whom the Cure2Children centers will offer operations.

Over time, we hope through our joint venture to reach out to every family that has a thalassemia sufferer, using the potential for a cure as a tool for education and prevention. In cases where an operation is not possible, our staff can help people learn about proper maintenance and care for their sick child. And when parents ask for an operation for their child, the staff will use this as an opportunity to promote screening: "We will provide testing for your child to determine whether a cure is possible. But in return, we ask that you bring your entire family in for genetic screening." In this way, information about thalassemia as well as wise practices for controlling the disease will gradually spread throughout Bangladesh.

✿ ✿ ✿

While preparations for our thalassemia units are under way, something else is happening in the mind of Dr. Lawrence Faulkner. He has been doing a lot of thinking about social business. "Already we have greatly reduced the amount of financial support we must provide to our centers in Pakistan," Dr. Faulkner reports. "In the first few months, we had to give them around 10,000 euros in donor money each month. Now the amount is just 5,000 euros. In time, these centers may be fully self-supporting. It would be wonderful if eventually all our projects around the world could be run as social businesses."

The goal of eliminating thalassemia is a realistic one. Something like 80 percent of patients achieve a complete cure when the bone marrow transplant is performed. Experience in Pakistan suggests that this rate is achievable in the developing world just as much as in Europe or America, especially since a transplant center can be established and maintained at a reasonable cost.

Dr. Faulkner and I both stress the value of running a social business on an "open source" basis. Social business—like the art of medicine itself—is all about solving problems, helping people, and making the world a better place. At its heart is the human quality of selflessness, rather than the selfishness that drives conventional business.

Thus, it makes sense for social business owners to look for opportunities to share information, ideas, and insights rather than hoarding them. Through conferences, publications, training programs, and teaching, Cure2Children plans to spread its knowledge about thalassemia and about the role of social business in healthcare to professionals and other interested partners around the world.

I hope every social business will share its expertise in the same spirit. After all, what good is creating a wonderful seed if you aren't willing to scatter it to the four winds?

CHAPTER 5

Legal and Financial Frameworks for Social Business

As I explained in Chapter 3, the most important first step in launching a social business is coming up with an idea. Usually this will grow from your observation of a social problem—something wrong that is causing human suffering in your own community or perhaps someplace else in the world. The natural reaction is to want to solve the problem, to relieve the suffering and ensure that it will never return. And here is where your creativity and ingenuity kick in. Can you devise a clever solution to the problem—one that is self-sustaining, is empowering, and promises a permanent cure rather than a temporary Band-Aid? If you think you have this kind of idea—or even if you have just the germ of an idea that needs further development and refinement—you may be ready to take the plunge into the world of social business.

Once you reach this point, it is time to think about how to fund your social business. Obtaining financing is probably one of the biggest hurdles you will have to face on the road to launching and running a successful social business. But with some creativity, resourcefulness, and a lot of patience, you should be able to achieve your goals.

This chapter will help you to navigate the multitude of resources available to assist you in your financing needs. As I'll explain, the question of financing is closely linked with the question of business structure. Companies and other organizations are governed by various legal and regulatory regimes, depending on the organization's exact form and purpose. And these differing sets of rules, in turn, have a big impact on your ability to raise money from specific sources. So part of our discussion in this chapter will be the choices you must make concerning the legal structure for your social business. As you'll see, these decisions will have a significant effect on the ways you raise money for launching, sustaining, and expanding the business.

One important step in the process of finding funding is creating a business plan that will help you in recruiting an investor network.

Creating a Business Plan to Attract Investors

Back in Chapter 3, I discussed several aspects of the business plan. As I explained, developing your business plan will probably be an ongoing process. You may create several versions of the plan—a preliminary one to give shape and detail to your business idea, for your own benefit and that of your initial partners, supporters, and friends; a more detailed plan for potential lenders and investors; and revised versions as your thinking evolves due to changing circumstances and learning. Changing and rewriting your business plan over time is natural and to be expected.

Since we're now focusing on the issue of attracting financial support, I'll discuss here some of the important issues related to a business plan for investors.

When you are ready to launch a full-blown social business that requires significant outside funding, you'll need to create a detailed budget for operationalizing your business. This can be done by creating a five-year financial forecast for your social business, including a robust cost structure that is broken down into various categories, including human resources (generally the largest expense), office space/ real estate needs, travel expenses, price of input materials, land and physical resources, and professional services.

The budget should also indicate the revenue structure, including the pricing of your business's service or product. If your idea is viable, your budget should indicate revenue flows that cover your expenses—preferably with a comfortable surplus to shield you from bad luck. Here is where many would-be entrepreneurs run into trouble. It is easy to be overly optimistic about the revenues you will generate, especially during the first year or two. Remember that it takes time for customers to learn about your new business, and even more time for them to change their buying habits and become your patrons. And unexpected competition can appear on the market at any time. The safest course is to estimate the level of sales you should be able to achieve during the first few years, and then cut it in half. It's very likely that the lower figure will prove to be more accurate. (And if you are lucky enough to achieve the higher target, congratulations! That will be a nice "problem" to have.)

Within your five-year forecast, focus on the cash flow statement. This reflects the actual movement of funds into and out of your company on a week-by-week, month-by-month basis. Some entrepreneurs make the mistake of considering their finances in balance if the end-of-the-year statement shows a balance between revenues and expenses. The end-of-year figures are important—but if you suffer a huge expense hit in April while revenues aren't due to arrive until September, your business may collapse over the summer. If you don't have personal expertise in accounting, consult with a professional who can ensure that your cash flow projections make sense and are accurate.

Developing a well-structured and detailed financial plan will help you to pinpoint exactly how much funding you will need and when you will need it. Beyond that, you are also developing a compelling storyline of who you are, what your skills, commitment, and background are, and how your social business will deliver an impact in the community you hope to serve.

Your budget should allow you to determine how much capital you will need to raise at the outset and how much you will need in total over the first five years. For the early days of a business, particularly the first eighteen months to three years of operation, the norm for start-up businesses is to spend far more cash than they generate. Eventually your goal should be to break even, but expect negative cash flow for some time as you secure reliable sources of funding for future operations. The amount of money that you will be spending each month (often referred to as your *burn rate*) dictates the amount of capital you will need as a bridge to the point where your social business is a self-sustaining operation.

Recruiting an Investor Network

Getting access to seed capital is vital to starting your business. At this stage, some key questions for you and your team to answer are: How should you structure your campaign for raising seed capital? Should you consider grants, debt, equity (that is, offering investors shares of ownership), or a mix of all three? What is the best approach to educate investors about the social value of your business? How will you demonstrate the potential or intended impact of the social business? How can you illustrate any innovative techniques or new ideas in your business model?

These questions will help you to develop a strategy for approaching potential investors. Based on this strategy, you will need to transform your detailed business and financial plans into a provocative presentation that will convey your key messages to investors quickly and effectively. Be as creative as you can. And ensure that your driving motivation and passion come through strongly in the presentation. Once these ingredients are in place, you are ready to begin utilizing the power of your personal network to connect with the right investors for your cause.

In most cases, start-up investments for a new social business will come directly from the founders' pockets or from networks of friends and family. Sometimes a few wealthy individuals, often called *angel investors,* will provide the capital you need to launch your business. But in other cases, your fund-raising success will depend on how effectively you can build a diverse network of contacts and resources. This process of networking will generally begin with people you know—friends, colleagues, classmates, business associates, community members, and people you think may be interested in the social problem you are addressing. In time, your networking will extend beyond personal contacts to include "friends of friends" and other acquaintances. High-tech communication tools such as Web sites, blogs, Twitter feeds, social networking sites, e-mail links, online newsletters and bulletin boards, and other similar connections can also help you find people who may want to support your effort.

One key factor that should be in place before you approach these networks is the management team. You should define clear roles for your leadership and designate specific management responsibilities for the various members of your team. When meeting with investors, you want to display competence and a solid management structure to let them know that you are well-placed to lead your business in the right direction. In addition, the business model is vital to showcase how your social business intends to produce social benefits and what processes it will follow in order to demonstrate potential impact, scale, and efficiency. You can also strengthen your case by showcasing results from your pilot program and/or customer feedback that indicate interest for the business' services.

Beyond your personal network, another potential source of funding for a new social business is the corporate social responsibility (CSR) funds that many companies, especially in Japan, now maintain. I'm a strong advocate of the idea that companies should use at least a portion of the CSR monies to help start social businesses rather than devoting it all to charitable causes (as is usually the case). This would be a more socially productive use of the money for the same reason that social business in general has an advantage over traditional charities:

Since a social business strives to be self-sustaining, there is the potential that money invested in a social business can generate benefits for society for years or decades to come. By contrast, money granted to a charity is generally spent within a few months—and the benefits, however great, tend to be limited.

If you decide to approach corporations in your community to suggest that they consider investing in your nascent social business, you should expect to spend some time educating them about this new concept. In time, as more and more people become aware of the power of social business, I predict that CSR fund managers will seek out promising social businesses and offer them financial help, even without being asked.

Eventually, other sources of financing for social businesses will emerge. In a later chapter, I'll describe the dedicated social business funds that are already springing up. In addition, socially responsible investment and pension funds, which are a popular and growing portion of the investment marketplace, may make it a practice to allocate a portion of their funds—say, 5 percent—to social businesses.

One final point about funding for a social business. Since a social business is dedicated to solving a social problem, it may attract foundation grants, charitable donations, and other gifts from organizations and people who want to help improve the world. Does accepting such grants disqualify a business from being a social business?

The answer is no. It's perfectly all right for a social business to accept a grant, provided it remains focused on the goal of becoming economically self-sufficient in a reasonable period of time. (An organization that relies on grants in perpetuity, of course, is not a social business but an NGO.) After all, traditional profit-maximizing companies receive grants from time to time, such as the tax breaks, land grants, and favorable government contracts often given to businesses. This doesn't disqualify them from being considered true businesses.

Grameen Bank itself received some grants in its earliest years. However, it has always been completely self-sufficient and has earned a profit every year but three years in its early history. Those who are starting social businesses today and are considering accepting grants for seed capital should follow the same model.

Various Legal Structures for Social Business

Over the past two years, I have devoted a lot of my time and energy to spreading the word about social business to audiences around the world. This book is part of that effort. So are the many speeches, presentations, interviews, and forums that I offer before groups of many kinds—business leaders, students, policy makers, NGO managers, foundation heads, and ordinary citizens from every walk of life. I am so convinced that social business is one key to addressing the most serious problems faced by humankind that I feel it is very urgent for me to communicate this concept to as many people as possible.

Unfortunately, our legal and regulatory systems do not currently provide a place for social business. Profit-maximizing companies and traditional non-profit organizations (foundations, charities, and NGOs) are recognized institutions covered by specific rules regarding organizational structure, governance and decision-making principles, tax treatment, information disclosure and transparency, and so on. But social business is not yet a recognized business category. This needs to change. The sooner there is a defined legal and regulatory structure for social business—preferably one with consistent rules in countries around the world—the easier it will be for entrepreneurs and corporations to create a multitude of social businesses to tackle the human problems that are plaguing society.

Until this gap in our legal system is filled, what options does the person or group interested in founding a social business have to choose from? In this section, I'll explain in general terms the existing possibilities and indicate what I think are the strengths and weaknesses of each. Naturally, if you are developing a social business concept, you'll want to consult with a knowledgeable attorney who is familiar with the national, state, and local regulations that apply to you.

The for-profit business structure. The best option today is to organize your social business under the traditional structure of a for-profit business. This means applying many of the same business principles that are used when developing an ordinary profit-maximizing company, while not losing sight of the social objective that should be at the heart of the enterprise. Of the increasing number of for-profit companies that claim a social mission, a handful go so far as to renounce the pursuit of profits that benefit the owners—which puts them on the threshold of qualifying as true social businesses.

The for-profit legal framework was used for all of Grameen's social businesses. Such a social business has a traditional ownership structure, which creates clear lines of power and responsibility. The for-profit company has a number of options for raising capital: It can solicit investments from individuals, companies, and investment funds; it can offer ownership shares for sale; and it can borrow money from banks and other lending institutions (providing it can demonstrate its financial stability and creditworthiness). Also, in most jurisdictions, the legal system gives the for-profit company great freedom and flexibility to experiment with its business model.

For-profit companies must pay taxes on any surplus they generate. Also, investments in for-profit companies—unlike donations to charities and some other kinds of non-profits—do not receive favorable treatment from the tax authorities. Thus, a social business organized as a for-profit company must be just as financially efficient as any other for-profit company, since it doesn't benefit from any tax breaks. (For reasons I'll explain later, I believe social businesses should be tax-paying entities.)

In many states and countries, there is an explicit or implicit rule that for-profit companies have a legal obligation to maximize profits for the benefit of their owners and investors. It's possible that the leaders of a social business could actually be sued for devoting some of the company's resources to socially beneficial purposes—for example, providing higher-than-market wages to employees from disadvantaged social groups, or offering goods and services at a discounted price to poor people.

It's possible that this risk can be minimized if the shareholders sign an upfront declaration renouncing their right to profit from the company beyond the return of their original equity investment. However, even if investors sign a statement that they know the company is a social business, that they will not take profit beyond the amount of their investment, the door always remains open so that investors may change their mind at any point in the future and decide that they want the company to switch from a social business into a company that generates profit for the shareholders. (After all, it was the shareholders' decision to create a social business; nobody forced them to do it, and they are free to change their minds.) It's easy to imagine this happening in a time of economic recession when shareholders are under financial strain, as well as at times of market boom when the company is making an attractive profit.

This risk that investors may decide to abandon the social business structure in favor of a traditional profit-maximizing structure is a potential drawback to using the legal structure designed for profit-maximizing companies. In the future, governments can and should create a separate law for social business, defining it adequately for regulatory purposes, and indicating the responsibilities and obligations of the shareholders. The law should lay down the rules and procedures a social business must follow in order to switch to a profit-maximizing company. At the same time, we should amend the existing company law to include the rules and procedures under which a profit-maximizing company can switch to a social business company.

Another disadvantage of the for-profit structure is that, under most legal regimes, it can be difficult for non-profit organizations such as foundations to invest in for-profit companies. This means that a foundation with a special interest in, say, promoting better healthcare may be discouraged from investing some of its funds in a social business that provides healthcare to the poor. Under U.S. law, foundations can invest in for-profit companies only if the investment qualifies as a "program-related investment" (PRI). Unfortunately, the rules defining PRIs are complicated, and violating them can lead to serious tax problems for the foundation. As a result, many foundations shy away from such investments.

The non-profit organizational structure. Many people have suggested to me that a social business might better be structured as a non-profit organization, like the typical charity, foundation, or NGO.

The idea that a non-profit organization might engage in business activities is not a new one. It has long been customary for certain kinds of non-profits to sell goods and services, using the revenues generated to maintain their operations, offer help to the poor and others who may not be able to afford to pay, and to produce other social benefits. Hospitals, schools, universities, arts institutions, and low-income housing providers are examples of non-profits that commonly engage in revenue-generating activities. In recent years, this model has been expanded by non-profit organizations that create goods and services specifically to benefit the poor.

Those who support the non-profit options point out that there is no expectation that a non-profit organization will produce a profit, so its managers are not likely to be besieged by angry donors demanding a return on their contribution. But this is not always true. For example, there are non-profit organizations that run microfinance programs in which international financial institutions have invested. These investors do expect high returns on their investments.

Depending on the exact nature of the non-profit, there may be favorable tax treatment of any donations or gifts received, which can help significantly in attracting such contributions. And non-profit organizations like foundations find it much easier to make grants to other non-profits than to invest in for-profit companies—even if the activities being performed and the social benefits created are almost the same.

However, there are also serious limitations to using the non-profit structure for social business. Perhaps the most significant is the strict legal and regulatory scrutiny that non-profits often experience. (That's the price they pay for the favorable tax treatment they enjoy.) In a 2009 article about the organizational choices facing what he calls "social enterprises," attorney Robert A. Wexler comments about the difficulty of winning tax-exempt, non-profit status for such organizations in the United States:

> Every exemption application that I have submitted for an organization that seeks to produce products or develop services to benefit the poor has received several rounds of I[nternal] R[evenue] S[ervice] questions. Why? In my view, the IRS questions are not at all out of line given the lack of authority in this evolving area. IRS exemption application reviewers typically have few concrete guidelines to help them when evaluating this type of exemption application, and they cannot be blamed for being cautious.*

Thus, if you try to launch a social business under the non-profit format, you should be prepared to answer tough questions, such as: How will the founders benefit from this organization? Can you demonstrate that the activities of the organization will be exclusively educational or charitable—or will private individuals be the main beneficiaries? And why should the government view the organization as noncommercial when it is engaging in activities that are usually considered commercial, such as the production and sale of goods or services? You'll have to answer these questions to the satisfaction of the

---

*Robert A. Wexler, "Effective Social Enterprise—A Menu of Legal Structures," *Exempt Organization Tax Review* 63, no. 6 (June 2009): 565–576.

tax authorities if you want your social business to qualify as a non-profit organization.

Furthermore, in some countries, including Bangladesh, the for-profit activities of a non-profit organization are subject to taxes, which eliminates any special tax advantage to this business structure.

Thus, under my definition of social business, there's no good fit with the non-profit structure. Remember, a Type I social business is a commercial organization in every sense—except that any surplus (or "profit") is not taken by the owners. Unlike a non-profit organization, which is sustainable only in very rare, exceptional cases, a social business always aims for sustainability. A social business has to be a business in the first place. By contrast, a non-profit is not designed as a business. It can only imitate business to the extent the current board wants to do so. Next year, a board with new members may change the rules. Under the circumstances, it's not realistic to expect a non-profit to follow all the business rules consistently.

The most important reason for not using the non-profit legal structure for creating a social business is that a non-profit is not owned by anyone; it can't issue shares. A social business has one or more owners, can issue shares, and can buy and sell shares, just like any for-profit company. Ownership is what makes social business so special. Owners take pride in what they are doing, what they are creating, and what results they are producing. They become personally involved in the company. Shares of social businesses can be inherited. Families will take pride in what their ancestors did to benefit the world. These companies will become part of the family heritage. Individuals and their families will take pleasure in creating and maintaining the legacy. In a non-profit, however, one can be involved only as a board member or as an employee. Once your term is over, you are no longer a part of the organization. There is no sense of legacy lending strength and permanence to the mission.

For all these reasons, the concept of social business that I have in mind does not fit into a non-profit legal format at all.

The non-profit linked to a for-profit company. It's not unusual for non-profit organizations to create for-profit subsidiaries that sell goods and services, and thereby produce income that goes to support the work of the non-profit parent. In other cases, non-profits create partnerships with for-profit companies that provide them with income they use for their social mission. A charity hospital that owns and operates a shopping mall might be an example of this kind of relationship.

One category of Type II social business is designed this way. In this category, we create a trust dedicated to the social objectives we have in mind. The trust will invest in a wholly-owned, or almost wholly-owned, for-profit company whose profits are used by the trust in achieving its social objectives. Success in achieving these objectives will be the measure of the success of the social business, which means that these social objectives have to be formulated in a measurable way.

In the discussion about for-profit and non-profit business structures, we always get drawn into the tax issue. In order to encourage charitable giving by individuals and companies, governments around the world have created various tax incentive packages, including generous tax exemptions. Many have suggested to me that social business should also be made tax-exempt. I cannot readily agree with this proposition. I see social business as an expression of spontaneous selflessness unconditioned by outside encouragement, particularly if that encouragement makes the investor a financial beneficiary.

I am in favor of creating a favorable environment for social business to blossom. For example, it's important to create social business funds to provide credit and equity to social business. However, mandating a tax-exempt status for social business may go too far. Suppose the government lets you take the dollar which was supposed to be handed over to the government as tax and invest it in a social business instead. Under the principles of social business, that dollar will come back to you, not to the government. This means you will financially benefit from the social business, thereby activating your selfish motivations, which are supposed to be irrelevant to investing in social business. I would rather keep social businesses as taxable entities rather than make selfish calculations part of the social business equation.

I want this issue to be seriously debated. Until a satisfactory resolution is reached, we can leave the door open for governments to take action on a case-by-case basis. Governments may decide from time to time that investments in particular social businesses should enjoy tax-exempt status under specific conditions and for a pre-determined time period. Similar decisions could be made with reference to the tax status of the surpluses earned by social businesses. This will enable governments to give various types of support to various kinds of social businesses, depending on social urgencies and government's need for revenue. For their part, social businesses can carry out their investment plans without waiting for government decisions on tax-exemption.

Emerging alternative structures. In recent years, there have been several experiments with new business structures that differ from both the traditional for-profit structure and the non-profit structure. In part, these new developments are a response to the same social forces that motivated me to create the concept of social business. Like me, many people feel frustrated by the narrow, limited options our current economic and political systems offer. Like me, many people have been searching for a new way to combine the creativity and dynamism of business with the idealism and selflessness of charity. Demands from these people have led some government jurisdictions to create new business formats that attempt to fill the void in the current system.

Unfortunately, none of the current experiments with new business structures match precisely my concept of social business—at least, none that I am aware of. But it is useful to compare these structures with social businesses in order to understand the differences clearly.

One of the alternative legal structures now emerging is the *community interest company* (CIC). This is a new legal vehicle for business available since 2005 in the United Kingdom for what the British government refers to as "social enterprises." According to the UK authorities, "CICs will be organisations pursuing social objectives, such as environmental improvement, community transport, fair trade etc. Social enterprises are playing an increasing role in regenerating disadvantaged areas, empowering local communities and delivering new, innovative services at local level."

In some ways, a CIC resembles a traditional charity. Like a charity, it is committed to providing benefits to the society rather than enriching owners or shareholders. A government regulator is responsible for examining each proposed CIC to make sure it passes what's called the Community Interest Test. This means satisfying the regulator that the purposes of the CIC "could be regarded by a reasonable person as being in the community or wider public interest." The benefits delivered by the CIC must also not be restricted to a very small or select group (to ensure that someone doesn't try to label a profit-maximizing company as a CIC by claiming that it has been created to provide "social benefits" to a specially defined group of insiders—such as the family and friends of the company founder).

The Community Interest Test that a CIC must pass is less strict than the rules a charity must meet in the UK. However, the CIC also doesn't enjoy the tax benefits that a charity gets. A CIC pays taxes on its revenues in much the same way as any ordinary business. Also, the assets held or generated by the CIC, including any surplus of revenues over expenses, are subject to what is called an asset lock. This is a legal requirement that the assets of the CIC be used solely for community benefits. For example, the assets can be used to directly benefit the community, to expand the work of the CIC, or as collateral for a loan that is needed to maintain or continue the work of the CIC. (There is one exception to the asset lock rule—a big one—that I'll explain in a moment.)

Like a profit-maximizing company, a CIC has one or more owners. A charity can own a CIC; so can an individual, a group, or another company. (A political party, however, is not permitted to own a CIC.)

A CIC can solicit funds from investors and it can even issue shares of stock, just like a traditional corporation. In this respect, a CIC is similar to my concept of a social business. (Grameen Danone and Grameen Veolia Water, for example, are both owned jointly by the Grameen companies and by their parent corporations—Danone and Veolia Water, respectively.)

However, unlike a social business, a CIC may pay dividends to shareholders (this is the exception to the asset lock rule), though these dividends are limited by law. Currently, the maximum dividend per share is 5 percent above the Bank of England base lending rate, and the total dividend declared in any given year is limited to 35 percent of the company profits.

One might conclude from this that a CIC is simply a special form of for-profit company, with all the limitations and disadvantages that such a company faces when trying to address social problems. The UK government explains its approach this way: "We think a balance can be struck between the flexibility needed by CICs to raise finance and the need to provide a meaningful asset lock. Although investors have the possibility of making a modest return, this will be restricted in order to ensure that the main beneficiary of the CIC is the wider community."

I've explained elsewhere my reasons for believing that it's crucial that social businesses *not* be subject to the expectations and pressures that naturally arise when the payment of dividends is part of the business plan. The "balance" that the UK authorities intend to pursue is generally quite elusive. The CIC is a restricted-profit company, and as such does not qualify to be the kind of social business that I have been promoting. Obviously, however, a CIC could become a social business if the owners and shareholders explicitly and clearly renounced the acceptance of dividends or any other form of profit distribution beyond the amount of investment.

The CIC concept is attracting widespread interest. As of the end of 2009, there were over 3,300 CICs registered in the UK. Some have become quite successful and well-known—for example, Firefly Solar, which uses sustainable technologies in producing events for organizations ranging from the Glastonbury Music Festival to Greenpeace; Eco-Actif Services, which provides employment training and counseling to ex-offenders, recovering addicts, single parents, and other at-risk individuals; and Zaytoun, a trading company that works with farm cooperatives in Palestine to produce and market fair trade–certified olive oil for sale in the UK.

There is also considerable discussion about creating a similar legal structure in Canada. For example, in November 2007, former prime minister Paul Martin delivered a lecture titled "Unleashing the Power of Social Enterprise" at the Munk Centre for International Studies in Toronto. Martin described the potential for good of businesses organized for social purposes and discussed the need of the Canadian government to respond to "the real world evolution of the social economy, that of social enterprise in its fullest sense." I hope this interest in the CIC will translate into support for social business.

Another new business structure that also reflects the quest for a way of harnessing the power of business for social purposes is the *low-profit limited liability company,* often called an L3C. A variation on the familiar business structure known as the limited liability company (LLC), the L3C idea was originated by Robert Lang, CEO of the Mary Elizabeth & Gordon B. Mannweiler Foundation. It has since been refined and promoted by Americans for Community Development, the Council on Foundations, the Social Enterprise Alliance, and other organizations looking for creative ways to combine for-profit techniques with social purposes.

The first law establishing the L3C structure was enacted by the state of Vermont in 2008. As of the end of 2009, the concept had also been recognized by Michigan, Utah, Wyoming, and Illinois, and legislation permitting the formation of L3C corporations was being considered in North Carolina, Georgia, Oregon, South Dakota, Tennessee, and Montana. The Crow Indian Nation and the Oglala Sioux Tribe also recognize the L3C structure.

The L3C, like the CIC, is fundamentally a for-profit company that pursues a social purpose. Like other businesses, an L3C has one or more owners, which can include individuals, charities, or for-profit companies. And like a CIC, an L3C can pay dividends on any financial surplus it generates. These dividends are expected to be low, since the laws creating L3Cs specify that "no significant purpose of the company is the production of income or the appreciation of property." However, there are no written guidelines limiting the size of profits (as there are with the CIC), and no public regulator is designated to pass judgment on whether a particular L3C is paying profits that are "excessive."

As with other limited liability companies, the L3C has a "pass-through" status in regard to U.S. federal income taxes. That is, the corporation itself pays no income tax. Instead, all items of income, expense, gain, and losses are "passed through" to the "members" (i.e., owners) of the L3C in proportion to their ownership shares.

One advantage of the L3C structure is that its founding requirements—the dedication to "charitable or educational purposes," the disavowal of profit as a "significant purpose," and the avoidance of "political or legislative purposes"—are all designed to mirror the U.S. Internal Revenue Code rules defining program-related investments (PRIs). Some of those who have advocated the legal establishment of the L3C structure have expressed the hope that this form of social enterprise will win the financial support of foundations, since L3Cs have been specifically designed to qualify, for legal and tax purposes, as legitimate PRIs that foundations can invest in. This is important to foundations, since, as I noted earlier, the Internal Revenue Service rules defining PRIs are famously complicated and difficult to follow. Having a "ready-made" business structure that qualifies as a PRI should encourage foundations to explore this option for investing some of their funds.

In addition to providing funding, foundations that support L3Cs can also create indirect financial benefits for the companies. Through a technique known as "tranching," the investments can be structured so that the foundation investors shoulder the greatest financial risk while demanding little or no profit. This makes the remaining shares more attractive to other investors, such as banks, insurance companies, or endowment funds, since they have relatively lower risk and greater potential for return.

It will be interesting to see how the L3C concept develops in the years to come. One area in which there has been much discussion of L3Cs has been journalism. With local newspapers facing serious financial woes thanks to the rise of the Internet and the consequent draining away of advertising dollars, some journalists have been searching for new ways to fund organizations dedicated to investigative reporting and the education of the citizenry. Now some are hoping that foundation-supported L3Cs will become a way of keeping traditional journalism alive.

One example is the Chicago News Cooperative, dedicated to providing high quality, professionally edited news and commentary to the Chicago region. Currently a non-profit, it is studying the new Illinois law and may incorporate as an L3C in the future. Edited by veteran journalist James O'Shea and operated in partnership with WWTW, Chicago's public television station, it has received a grant from the John D. and Catherine T. MacArthur Foundation and is hoping for further investments from foundations. (The chair of the co-op's advisory board, Peter Osnos, founded PublicAffairs and has been my publisher as well as my friend.)

The legal and financial structure of the L3C makes it possible for an organization like a foundation to invest money in a business with social purposes and recover its initial investment, while eschewing, if it chooses, any further return. However, the big difference between the L3C and the social business is the same as with the CIC—the creation of profits to benefit owners and the payment of dividends from those profits are part of the agenda of the L3C, while they are deliberately excluded from the concept of the social business. In my judgment, making selfishness and selflessness work through the same vehicle will serve neither master well. The equivocation between the profit motive and the social motive introduces a weakness that will make the L3C less effective in its pursuit of humanitarian goals than the pure social business.

A third new concept in structuring a social business is the so-called *B corporation*. In reality, the name "B corporation" carries no special legal status; there is no law defining the B corporation or specifying any special regulations that apply to it. The idea of the B corporation was created by an organization called B Lab, which was founded in June 2006 by a young social entrepreneur named Coen Gilbert. Sensing the lack in ordinary economic and social thinking of a descriptive term for a business that has social goals as well as financial ones, Gilbert came up with the name B corporation using the analogy of C and S corporations, which are legal structures named after specific provisions in the U.S. tax code. However, the B in B corporation doesn't refer to the tax code—instead, it stands for "beneficial," since a B corporation is supposed to provide benefits to the community in which it operates.

If the B corporation has no real legal status, what is the purpose of creating the term? Gilbert and his associates at B Lab are trying to carve out a place in the economic system for a company that dedicates all or part of its profits to social causes. According to the rules established by B Lab, a company that wants to be "officially" designated a B corporation must include language in its governing documents (for example, its articles of incorporation, partnership agreement, or company bylaws) that specifically states that company directors may consider not just the financial interests of shareholders but also the welfare of many other "stakeholders," such as employees, customers, the community, and even the natural environment. The idea is to formally acknowledge the company's responsibilities to society alongside its economic responsibility to make a profit for investors—and thereby shield the company's managers and directors from legal attacks or investor rebellion when they make choices that benefit society while possibly diminishing profits.

In addition, B Lab offers a rating system that allows companies to measure their own environmental and social performance by answering a series of survey questions. The results yield a point score, and only companies that achieve a "passing" score (currently set at 80 out of a possible 200) are eligible to be designated as B corporations. The goal is to make the B corporation "brand" into a valuable form of recognition that enables everyone—customers, investors, employees, and the general public—to recognize companies that have made a real commitment to environmental and social sustainability.

Unfortunately, no one really knows whether the B corporation concept will be effective in achieving its primary goal—to win company managers and directors the freedom to run their businesses with social goals as well as financial ones. As one journalist (Ilana DeBare of the *San Francisco Chronicle*) puts it, "It's too early to know how much legal cover the B corporation language will really offer firms . . . if, for instance, they are sued by an unhappy investor who doesn't like their social or philanthropic priorities." DeBare goes on to note, "The situation is muddied further by the fact that some states have laws allowing companies to consider the interests of constituencies other than shareholders, while others including California don't have laws explicitly addressing that."*

Despite this uncertainty, some entrepreneurs have embraced the B corporation idea. As of the end of 2009, there were over two hundred B corporations in the United States. At this time, the value of this designation must be regarded as speculative.

And I must emphasize that a B corporation—even one with a very high score on the environmental and social survey created by B Lab—is *not* the same as a social business. A B corporation proclaims its concern about social goals, which I think is a fine thing. But each B corporation makes its own decisions about the role of profit. Rather

---

*Ilana DeBare, "'B Corporation' Plan Helps Philanthropic Firms," *San Francisco Chronicle*, May 18, 2008.

than renouncing the pursuit of personal gain, as the managers of a social business do, the managers of a B corporation are free to pay dividends to shareholders and to claim a share of the company profits for themselves. As I've explained, this seems to me to weaken the power of the B corporation concept—perhaps fatally.

The existence of these new, alternative forms of business structure—the CIC, the L3C, and the B corporation—reflects the same global situation that has driven my work in recent decades: the persistence of worldwide humanitarian problems that existing non-profit and for-profit organizations have failed to solve, and the void in our current economic and legal systems where a third form of business entity ought to be recognized. That these new alternatives have been devised, and that so many people are rushing to experiment with them, indicates that many people around the world share my desire to solve these problems. In that sense, I consider these experiments a hopeful sign. But I remain convinced that the social business concept, with its clear demarcation of a dividing line between the pursuit of profit and the pursuit of social goals, is the best way to complete the unfinished structure that is contemporary capitalism.

Obviously there is a lot of work to be done by our governmental, legal, and legislative experts. A new regulatory structure specifically tailored to the needs of social business should be created—the sooner the better. Meanwhile, those interested in launching social businesses will need to use the existing business laws as the basis for creating a true social business as I define it.

CHAPTER 6

Grameen Veolia Water

A Social R&D Project for
Addressing the World Water Crisis

Pragmatism, openness, experimentation—these have always been important elements in my approach to social business. The most important part of the process of setting up a social business is to define the end in the clearest terms. Means can be experimented with to get to the end. The goal of social business is to solve real-world problems and to help human beings live better, fuller lives. As long as a social business keeps this goal firmly in its sights, then the specific methods used to achieve the goal can be expected to evolve and change over time, as circumstances change and as better ideas emerge.

A very interesting illustration of this bias toward pragmatism can be seen in the story of Grameen Veolia Water. The second experiment in social business created by a major corporation, coming on the heels of Grameen Danone, Grameen Veolia Water is dedicated to providing pure drinking water to poor people in the village of Goalmari in Bangladesh.

The goal of the project: to develop a way to provide access to safe drinking water for rural Bangladeshis who now have to drink water contaminated with unacceptable levels of arsenic. The presence of this toxin in the water, which occurs naturally in the Himalayan alluvial soil of Bangladesh, was not discovered by scientists until 1993. It is associated with serious long-term health risks, including skin lesions and cancer, which afflict at least 100,000 people in my country. Currently millions of residents of Bangladesh are drinking arsenic-laden water every day, most of them in rural areas. The exact number affected by this problem is not known, but estimates range from 35 million to 80 million.

We have been trying to address this problem by undertaking various programs under Grameen Shikkha (Education). Nurjahan Begum, CEO of Grameen Shikkha, has been very passionate about bringing clean water to the villages. She and her team collected samples and studied maps showing various levels of arsenic in the tube-well water throughout Bangladesh, and they tried every solution proposed by experts, including filtration, rainwater harvesting, treating surface water with alum, and providing water through deep tube-wells. None of them solved the problem.

We are not the only ones who have tackled this challenge. The World Bank and other donors have been studying this problem for years and have allocated large sums of money to address it. UNICEF, which was blamed for having urged people in Bangladesh to switch from polluted surface water to water from hand-tube-wells that turned out to be arsenic-laden, applied all its capacities to the search for a solution. But no solution emerged.

In 2007, Eric Lesueur, an executive in the French company Veolia Water, came to see me with the question: Is there a social business that we can create together to improve the quality of the water available to the poor people of Bangladesh? I immediately dismissed the idea. I thought he was talking about bottled water, which is already popular in Bangladesh but also very expensive. It cannot supply the water needs of the massive rural population. But Lesueur did not give up. He stayed in Bangladesh and continued to make efforts to talk to me.

Finally, I told Lesueur through my office that if he thought he could deliver water to the villages at a cost of just one taka for ten liters, I would be willing to talk to him. There was silence from his side for two days. I thought he'd left Bangladesh. But then he contacted me again. "Yes," he said, "I can do that." I was pleasantly surprised and immensely interested in talking to him. This is how Grameen Veolia Water was born.

Veolia Water is part of a bigger company, Veolia Environment, which operates waste management systems, energy efficiency systems, public transportation systems, and water systems. Veolia Water, which focuses on the design, construction, and management of water and wastewater services for municipal and industrial clients, had 2008 revenues of some 12.6 billion euros, up almost 15 percent from the previous year.

Before Lesueur joined the Veolia Water team in 2006, he was deputy manager of R&D of global Veolia Environment. In this role, he became deeply interested in environmental management systems and the issues surrounding sustainable development, especially in relation to water supply.

Technology alone cannot solve the major challenges facing the world today. Selecting the social issues and picking the right technologies to address them are equally important. Social business can play an important role in addressing these challenges. At its root, social business is about making the economy work for everyone, including the poor people at the bottom of the pyramid who are usually left out. And here is where the companies like Veolia Water come in. How do you bring clean, safe drinking water to people whose incomes cannot support the costly infrastructure that may be involved? How do you adapt the new service to the customs and expectations that are part of their traditional way of life?

These questions and others like them turn out to be extraordinarily important, complex, and fascinating. Lesueur's mandate, according to company CEO Antoine Frérot, was to find ways for Veolia Water to make important contributions to answering these types of questions—not just in the developing world, but everywhere.

It has been clear for some time that water will be a central focus of sustainability issues all around the planet in the decades to come. Today, about 20 percent of the world's inhabitants have inadequate access to clean water for drinking and cooking. Experts say about 2 million children die every year due to water-related diseases, ranging from severe diarrhea to malaria and cholera. And these problems are expected to become worse. Thanks in part to global warming, many scientists predict that by 2025 half of the world's population may suffer from water shortages.

This problem has set off warning bells around the globe. The UN's Millennium Goals—eight international development goals that 192 United Nations member states and at least 23 international organizations made a commitment to achieve by the year 2015—include a focus on providing access to clean water for all the people of the world. (Specifically, Millennium Goal 7 commits the nations of the world to "reduce by half the proportion of people without sustainable access to safe drinking water and basic sanitation.")

Access to clean water is also an issue of women's rights. In African villages, for example, women and children usually are given the job of fetching water for the family. And in many places where a supply of water is not easily accessible, this means a job that may consume hours out of the day—carrying heavy pots or cans a distance of several miles to get to a well, pump, or river, and then carrying an even heavier container filled with water back to the farm or village. For many women, the ability to create a family business or to have a money-earning job is completely eliminated by the need to spend half the day fetching water; for many children, this task makes it impossible to attend school.

Furthermore, the problem of having access to clean drinking water is worse for women and their children than for men, particularly in countries like Bangladesh where men have greater freedom to travel outside the home because of cultural factors. In many villages of Bangladesh, the men spend part of the day in local shops or stores where they can drink clean water. Meanwhile, their wives and children are at home with access only to contaminated water from the local well or stream.

So creating a supply of clean drinking water is a health issue, an economic development issue, and a women's rights issue.

As he embarked on his new role of exploring ways for Veolia Water to develop social innovations around water supply, Eric Lesueur entered discussions with various organizations, including the Paris-based Association for the Development of Economic Initiatives (whose French acronym is ADIE). ADIE is run by a woman of great talent and energy named Maria Nowak, who happens to be a friend of mine and a pioneer of microcredit in France. Through Nowak, Lesueur learned that I would be traveling to Paris in March 2007 to visit ADIE and attend a conference. And Lesueur's attendance at this conference, where he heard me talk about the concept of social business, sparked in him the idea of launching a social business to bring clean water to the people of Bangladesh.

Lesueur's first step, even before consulting with us at Grameen Bank, was to share the idea with his colleagues at Veolia Water, especially Patrick Rousseau, who is CEO of Veolia Water's activities in the Indian subcontinent and is based in Delhi, India. Looking back on the experience, Lesueur notes the importance of enlisting a few key allies early in the process of launching a social business within a big company. "If I had been alone," he says, "even with the support of the top management of the company, it would have been difficult to make it work."

Here is a useful lesson for people who want to launch a social business: *A manager in a large company can get a social business initiative off the ground, provided he or she lays the right groundwork for it— which includes getting other people in the company excited about the project from the beginning.*

Lesueur arranged a trip to Dhaka in September 2007, accompanied by Rousseau and Estelle Lasselin, a colleague from Veolia Water's financial department. They met with me, and of course I was intrigued by the idea of creating a new social business in collaboration with such a large and experienced corporation. I sensed that they were serious about addressing the social challenges of supplying water for poor people and were ready to invest time, energy, and capital in learning about and experimenting with this new model of business. (On this same trip, they also visited the Grameen Danone yogurt plant in Bogra.)

So after Lesueur decided he could meet my ten-liters-for-one-taka challenge, we tentatively agreed to begin planning a Grameen-Veolia Water joint venture. It was the beginning of what would prove to be an interesting and complex journey together.

❊ ❊ ❊

When Lesueur got back to Paris, he described the proposed project to his CEO, Antoine Frérot. They held a two-hour conversation about the concept of social business, the problem of arsenic in the drinking water in Bangladesh, and the potential for a collaboration with Grameen. Frérot gave the project his enthusiastic blessing.

Lesueur also called Emmanuel Marchant of Danone and told him that Veolia Water was about to join Danone in the ranks of corporations supporting the social business concept. It was the first contact in what would become an ongoing exchange of ideas and experiences between these two companies.

In December 2007, a memorandum of understanding was signed between Grameen Healthcare and Veolia Water during my visit to Paris. The new project was now officially under way.

People in the business world often wonder how their colleagues will respond to the idea of social business. After all, a professional who has spent many years learning how to run an organization devoted to maximizing profit might be expected to be puzzled by or even hostile to the concept of investing in a project that is deliberately designed *not* to produce profits for the investors. But the reality is very different. At Veolia Water, just as it happened at Danone, people were excited and energized by the idea of collaborating with Grameen on this new form of business. Lesueur recalls, "I was amazed. Many people came up to me in the hallways to talk about the project, to offer their support, and even to volunteer to work on it with us in Bangladesh. The enthusiasm was extraordinary."

Actually, I don't find this surprising. It matches the response I encounter whenever I speak about social business. The desire to help make the world a better place and to improve life for our fellow human beings is just as strong a part of human nature as the drive to pile up personal profit. It's only natural that people in business who have suppressed this altruistic side of themselves for many years because of the gross flaw in the theoretical structure should be excited about the opportunity to express it.

Furthermore, the concept of social business was especially important for Veolia Water because of the company's place in the world economy. With Veolia Water already supplying drinking water to over 6.5 million people in India and Africa, the nations of the developing world are an important future market for its services and expertise. And in a time when water shortages, climate change, and controversies over economic globalization and the privatization of water supply services are creating political and economic challenges for Veolia Water, it's important for the company to play a positive role in the social issues around water.

As Antoine Frérot puts it:

Many people misunderstand the role of Veolia Water. We do not sell water. Anybody can take a bucket, dip it into the Seine, the Nile, or the Brahmaputra, and get water. Our business is to treat the water so that people can drink it safely. In other cases, where there is no water available, we find ways to bring it to the people.

But because people don't understand what we do, we are sometimes attacked in the media. It's painful for our people, who work hard to provide good services to people, doing everything from developing new means of water purification to spending weekends fixing water pumps and repairing leaks. So when we became committed to creating a social business for Bangladesh, it was exciting for our employees—a real breath of fresh air. Veolia Water and its people want to make positive contributions to the social issues around water, and this is a wonderful opportunity to do that.

I believe that Veolia Water hopes to gain knowledge and insights from this new project that will be applicable elsewhere in the developing world. It's no accident that Lesueur came from the R&D side of the company. Nor was it by chance that we decided together to launch a modest pilot project rather than trying to immediately solve the problems of 35 million people suffering from arsenic-tainted water in Bangladesh. Our real goal is to create a sustainable, self-supporting clean water system for a rural village in Bangladesh, learn how such a system can work and how it can be duplicated. If we can achieve that, the potential for social benefit is enormous.

Anybody can see that the challenge of supplying water to poor villagers is of vital importance to the future of Veolia Water's core business. This is one important difference between the Grameen Veolia Water project and the Grameen Danone project. Unlike yogurt, it's not possible to live without water. This creates enormous political, psychological, social, and economic issues and pressures on Veolia Water. The company's customers are usually public authorities that ask Veolia Water to provide water to everyone in a city, rich and poor alike. For example, Veolia Water's contract with the city of Tangiers in Morocco covers both the affluent districts where the pipes are new and sound and the poor districts where they are old and decayed. Both kinds of areas must be served.

Here, then, is another lesson for companies that are considering starting a social business: *Look to your core business, not a peripheral one, as a source of inspiration.* The more closely a social business relates to the parent company's own most basic interests, the more exciting and challenging the social business becomes to the company. This will ensure that it gets the attention, resources, and support it needs rather than being neglected or abandoned, especially when economic times are tough.

Under its various contracts with public authorities in Europe, South Asia, Africa, and other regions of the world, Veolia Water has been working to develop solutions to the challenge of providing affordable and sustainable water supplies to poor districts. Many approaches have been tried and found useful in particular settings.

One solution is to subsidize service to the poor areas through profits earned from sales of service to the rich areas. This is the "cross-subsidizing" approach that Grameen Healthcare uses when it charges differing rates for operations in its eye hospitals depending on the ability of patients to pay. It's also the same approach that Grameen Danone uses, in a different way, when it charges a higher price for its yogurt in urban areas than in rural villages.

Another solution is to subsidize water distribution in poor areas through the profits earned from selling electrical service when the same company happens to operate both electricity and water systems (as Veolia Water does in Gabon, for example).

Yet another is to find technical solutions that streamline both the delivery and payment systems—for example, prepaid electronic access cards for tap points. Veolia Water's water-delivery standpipe system, called Saqayti—"my fountain" in Arabic—has used this system very effectively.

And Veolia Water has also worked with local authorities to develop still other means of financing water supply for the poor, including local taxes (which spread the costs over a broader population) and the use of microcredit to pay for local supply systems. All these solutions have been implemented through public/private partnerships in various places in Africa, chiefly in urban areas. This history of social and economic experimentation lay behind Veolia Water's enthusiasm for testing the new model of social business.

❊ ❊ ❊

Under the joint venture agreement establishing Grameen Veolia Water (GVW), Veolia Water and Grameen Healthcare worked together to develop the business model for Bangladesh. The process began when Veolia Water came to Grameen and said, "Tell us where we should launch our project. We need a place where there's a real arsenic problem; a place not too far from Dhaka; and a place where people will be enthusiastic and supportive." After some internal discussion and debate, Grameen suggested a location for the first pilot project: the village of Goalmari, some fifty kilometers (around thirty miles) east of Dhaka, where about 20,000 local people could be served.

As I've mentioned, Veolia Water has significant experience in providing water services to people in the developing world, including poor people, but the company's existing contracts are almost all in urban settings. Bringing water to people in a Bangladeshi village poses very different challenges. The population density is low, and seasonal changes between the dry and rainy seasons, which completely transform the landscape, create significant technical difficulties for a water supply project.

Even more important, however, are the social and economic challenges of rural Bangladesh. GVW had to find ways to integrate its new water supply service into the social structure of the village, attracting far-flung customers from various income levels and convincing people to spend money on a product they have traditionally received for free—though at a cost to their families' long-term health.

The complementary nature of our joint venture was clear from the outset. Veolia Water provided the technical expertise, while Grameen provided the relationships with the local people and the understanding of social and economic conditions. Together with the members of the GVW team, I visited Goalmari several times to meet with the people, to explain our social business concept, to describe why the new water supply system was important for them, and to explain the role of Veolia Water—this French company that few people in Bangladesh were then familiar with. GVW also conducted a first assessment of how many people in the village were likely to buy water, using a group of local students to perform a very simple house-to-house survey.

For its part, Veolia Water moved quickly, launching the project in March 2008, just three months after we'd signed the memorandum of understanding. Antoine Frérot explains:

> Rather than spend months studying the economics of the project and designing the plant, we decided to quickly find a location, to buy the land, and to start work immediately, learning as we went along.
>
> This learn-by-doing approach was made possible by the fact that the initial project is modest in size, requiring only a small investment. Rather than spending millions of euros on a large-scale facility, and perhaps losing the entire investment, we decided to start small and to learn on the fly. We consider it R&D spending and therefore we are prepared to spend in the interest of acquiring knowledge.

Here is an important lesson for others interested in starting social businesses: *There's a huge advantage to starting small.* When you start small, you can start quickly—and this enables you to learn from your mistakes, change direction, and steadily improve. My experience in launching the various Grameen businesses is that this is the most effective way to create truly innovative companies. It's also very creative, exciting—and a lot of fun!

The technical problems of supplying water to a rural area proved to be amenable to systems that Veolia Water had developed previously. In Bangladesh, Veolia Water is treating surface water drawn from the Meghna River rather than the groundwater traditionally accessed by shallow wells. This decision was made because groundwater treatment is considerably more expensive and creates waste-disposal problems that don't exist when surface water is used. The purification process is a familiar one, employing activated carbon filtration and chlorination. The main new element was the need to adapt this type of system to serve a rural area with a small-capacity plant (just ten cubic meters, around thirty-five cubic feet, per hour), since people have to use the filtered water only for drinking and cooking. (Water contaminated with arsenic seems to be safe for washing and other sanitary purposes.)

Veolia Water considered two different technical models for the water-treatment plant. One was to build a fixed plant with a concrete base; the other was to use small mobile units, like those employed in emergency situations, to bring water to refugees in rural encampments. In the end, Veolia Water chose to build a fixed plant.

The target price for selling the treated water was the one I initially suggested to Veolia Water—one taka for ten liters when purchased at the plant. But water sold elsewhere in the village had to be priced higher, since creating and maintaining the network of pipes that transport the water adds to the cost. There's also a need to provide a profit margin to the dealers who sell the water—a team of local women, "Grameen ladies," currently eleven in number, who sell the water to their friends and neighbors in the village. Believing the villagers were resistant to the idea of fixing different prices for the same product at different locations, Grameen Veolia Water decided to charge three taka for ten liters across the board.

Grameen Veolia Water estimates that the typical household needs about thirty liters of water per day for drinking and cooking, which would translate into a daily cost of around nine taka—not an insignificant amount for a poor family in Bangladesh, but affordable for most.

GVW built the plant together with a network of pipes and tap points, two kilometers (a little more than a mile) in radius, to make pure water available at some fourteen convenient locations around the village. The plant began to operate in March 2009, and the network swung into action in June. It was manned by a team of six local Bangladeshis, hired and trained by GVW, supplemented by a single French technician. In case of any difficulties, the Veolia Water office in India was available for consultations and assistance.

From a technical standpoint, everything worked beautifully. We were all excited when the first stream of pure, filtered water began to flow from the GVW treatment plant. It was thrilling to see local men, women, and children lining up outside the plant and at the various tap points with their own clay or metal jugs and bottles, eager to sample the new, more healthful beverage. The people of Goalmari finally had access to drinking water that would not make them sick.

But then the real challenges faced by Grameen Veolia Water began to become clear.

❄ ❄

Within days, the GVW team discovered that most residents of the village were not very keen to buy water—despite the enthusiasm they had expressed, no doubt sincerely, when surveyed by our student team.

The monthly sales figures tell the tale. The question is—why?

The GVW team is working to answer this question and develop solutions. What follows are the tentative explanations they have come up with so far.

It appears that the resistance within the village comes from a couple of sources. Price is one big problem. Marketing the water at the higher price set by GVW attracted daily sales of only around 2,500 liters, which means that just 10 to 15 percent of the target population was being reached.

A second problem is the fact that many—not all—of the villagers are unaccustomed to paying for water. One exception is when people—mostly men—buy drinking water by the glass in local restaurants, cafés, or shops. The going rate is 1 taka per glass, which is much higher than the rate at which GVW sells its water. But when it comes to consuming water at home, most Bangladeshis don't recognize the need or the economic sense to buying water.

Third, the health risk posed by the arsenic in the drinking water is hard to recognize. It's a long-term danger as opposed to an immediate one, since it takes years for people to develop lesions or cancers. The local people don't see anyone getting sick quickly after drinking the water, and it tastes all right. As a result, they don't fully accept that there's a need to buy pure water. Even those who understand that arsenic poses health risks don't really take the problem seriously enough. Some may think, "Well, this water may make me sick in twenty years. But who knows? In twenty years I might be dead anyway. So why worry about it?"

This is not a problem peculiar to people in Bangladesh. It's a problem of human nature. Many experiments and studies by economists, sociologists, and psychologists show that people from every culture find it very difficult to take long-term considerations as seriously as short-term, immediate ones. This is why affluent, well-educated people in Europe and America often have problems dealing with overeating, drinking, and smoking: The "bad" activities often provide quick gratification, while the health damage takes years to be apparent.

Finally, not all of the local people are affected equally by the arsenic problem. Some people who are relatively affluent can dig tube wells over one hundred meters (three hundred feet) deep, which yield arsenic-free water. Only about 25 percent of the tube wells in Goalmari meet the World Health Organization standards, but these wells do exist, mitigating the water quality problem for the families that have access to this pure water.

What can be done to address these issues? Solutions need to be found if GVW is to become a successful, self-sustaining social business—and, more important, if the water-drinking habits of the people of Goalmari are to be improved so that arsenic no longer produces needless illnesses.

The GVW team has been searching for these solutions. In 2010, a new strategy was approved by the board of GVW. Since demand for water from the plant is insignificant at the price offered to the villagers, and 95 percent of the plant capacity remains unutilized, why not bottle the water in 20-liter jars for institutional buyers? Profit earned in that segment of the market could be passed to the rural consumers by way of a very low price. Our goal will be to bring the price down to one taka per ten liters as originally conceptualized, and to expand the rural network to reach out to many more villages.

A second strategy would be to provide water to a cluster of households without going through dealers. And still another strategy would be to provide a direct in-home water supply to relatively affluent villagers—that is, to those who can afford to pay to have a link to the network of pipes installed and then pay for the water they use each month.

We intend to continue to pursue our original action plan—to bring water to the rural villagers at the lowest possible price so as to address the health issues and the social issues related to pure, healthy water. Now it is obvious that cross-subsidization will be an important part of the equation—selling water at higher prices to those who can afford it as a way of reducing the costs to the poor. As we develop a range of marketing programs for selling water to many kinds of customers, it may be that we will create a global system for sustainable water supply that can be applicable elsewhere in the developing world.

It's easy to see some similarities to the Grameen Danone story. One of the challenges for the yogurt business was finding distribution channels for the product. It took time and experimentation to figure out how to combine differing marketing programs, including local Grameen ladies distributing the yogurt door to door, sales directly at the plant, sales in local shops, and sales in urban stores. A similar array of distribution channels, each appropriately priced, will probably need to be developed to make the water business viable—although GVW is just at the beginning of this process.

Of course, there is one big difference from the perspective of the companies involved. Groupe Danone already sells its products to end customers through supermarkets around the world, so the company is very good at marketing. Veolia Water, on the other hand, does not normally sell goods or services directly to consumers. So some of the marketing methods that Grameen Danone has used, from creating a retail network to television advertising, are part of Danone's core business—but they are brand-new to Veolia Water.

But GVW is taking on the challenge. The goal is to develop a viable multichannel marketing and distribution system during 2010—one that hopefully will be replicable in other villages. On this basis, GVW can then begin planning expansion into other parts of Bangladesh that also need healthy drinking water.

✿ ✿ ✿

As you see, the story of Grameen Veolia Water is very much a work in progress. By the time this book is published, there are likely to be new twists and turns in the tale. Several milestones loom on the road ahead. During 2011, a second water-purification plant in another village will be established. The goal is to build three more plants by 2012 with a target of 100,000 people served. Current long-term estimates are that a total investment of around $250 million would meet the arsenic challenge for the entire nation of Bangladesh—a very modest sum for such a major health problem.

At the same time, experimentation with the business model will continue. My rule is very clear: *Always keep the goal in mind, but ad-*

just your methods as circumstances and new learning dictate. In this case, as long as the central goal of bringing an affordable, sustainable supply of healthy drinking water to poor people is kept in focus, there's no problem with testing many ways of making the project economically viable.

As with Grameen Danone, outside help is being employed to study and measure the social impact of the project and, we hope, to validate its benefits. A local laboratory, clinical, and research organization with special expertise in diarrheal diseases and arsenic contamination, ICDDR,B, is working with GVW technical staff to survey the water-usage habits of the residents of Goalmari and estimate the health benefits the project creates. As the results of this study begin to emerge, we will share them with the world and, of course, we will use them to guide our planning for future improvements in the business.

Back in Paris, one of the challenges faced by Eric Lesueur and CEO Antoine Frérot is justifying the continued investment in GVW. While enthusiasm for the concept of social business remains strong, a few people within Veolia Water wonder why the company is supporting a social business that eschews profit in Bangladesh, while in neighboring India—another country with millions of poor people—Veolia Water operates on a traditional profit-maximizing basis. But there is nothing surprising about the coexistence of social business and profit-making business within the same company. Each of these businesses has a different objective, but they learn from each other continuously. I am sure that after we go through our learning process in Bangladesh, Veolia Water will be launching social businesses in India, too. The only problem for the company is to develop creative ways to keep the two markets separate. There is no reason why one segment of the population has to be totally ignored for the sake of "protecting" the profit-making potential of the company. If people die of water pollution, get sick because of arsenic contamination, or remain poor because of health conditions, there is no future for profit-making. When social business can address all these problems, there is a better future for profit-making, too.

I am sure Veolia Water takes the GVW project very seriously. It's not simply a pet project of the CEO of Veolia Water—the expression of a purely private interest, like an art collection or a stable of race horses. It's part of the long-term vision for Veolia Water worldwide. As Lesueur explains:

> There must be a price for water if water supply is to be sustainable. The questions are: What should that price be? How should it be set? How can the society organize water supply to make sure that everyone, including the poorest, can afford it? We want to approach these questions in a very pragmatic way, not an ideological one. And we believe that social business can be an important part of the answer.

Social business and profit-making businesses both can play an essential and beneficial role in meeting the world's water needs. Partnerships between private companies and public authorities, who represent the people, are familiar around the world. I am introducing social business as a new option. Both public authorities and profit-making companies can create social businesses to address the problem of providing safe water to people who otherwise would remain vulnerable in the absence of safe water. We need all the creativity we can muster to solve this massive social problem. If creative social businesses can contribute in addressing this problem, that will be a big help.

Our experiment in Bangladesh will help test that idea and, we believe, show its value. And since the issue of social affordability for water is going to be a problem of increasing importance in the coming decades, experiments like this one are crucial.

This is why we wish to proceed with the Goalmari project with such urgency—not only for the benefit of the people of Goalmari but also for the benefit of the social business concept, which the world needs so badly.

So the Goalmari project is an important social experiment—a "social R&D project" whose initial success in economic and business innovation will open the door for many improvements that will bear fruit around the world in the years to come.

CHAPTER 7

Creating a Global Infrastructure for Social Business

Once I had formulated the idea of social business and begun to sense its potential for changing the world, I realized that I needed allies and supporters to turn it from an idea into a reality.

Fortunately, the worldwide attention received by Grameen Bank and microcredit provided me with a platform that I could use to explain the concept of social business to a large audience. *Creating a World Without Poverty* became very useful in explaining the concept in greater detail. Luckily, the book became a bestseller. As people around the world began to read it, I started receiving support from many quarters.

One set of supporters was the business leaders who were intrigued by the social business concept and eager to try it out. I've already told you the stories of some of these experiments, including Grameen Danone and Grameen Veolia Water, and I will be sharing more of them later in the book.

Another important group of supporters has been people from the world of non-profits, NGOs, foundations, and charities. Many of them have come to see social business as a valuable new tool for promoting global change in a sustainable, scalable way. Dr. Lawrence Faulkner and Eugenio La Mesa are an example of this category.

But in addition to what I might call "social business practitioners"—people and organizations that are actually launching social businesses—there's an important class of people emerging who may be described as "social business thinkers." These are people and organizations dedicated to studying and exploring the ideas behind social business, and to teaching the world about them. They form a kind of "intellectual infrastructure" for social business, adding depth, detail, and insight to my original concept and addressing many of the questions and challenges it raises.

I've been very pleased by the speed with which the social business idea has penetrated the worlds of academia and scholarship. A number of institutions have already created academic positions and units dedicated to offering courses; investigating and disseminating ideas about social business; serving as a bridge between professors, students, and businesses; and connecting the realm of thinking and visioning with the realm of action. These initiatives are significant because they indicate ready recognition of a new concept at the highest academic levels. The business world finds it easy to adopt the concept because of the respectability the scholars provide to it. They are serving as vital catalysts for encouraging social business experimentation.

The Yunus Centre

The Yunus Centre was established in August 2008 to serve as the anchor of all Grameen-related social businesses worldwide as well as many social business institutions around the world. Headed by Lamiya Morshed, the Centre is located at Grameen headquarters in Dhaka, Bangladesh. This gives it the opportunity to use Grameen resources in helping to establish social businesses, as most Grameen companies are only an elevator ride away!

The Yunus Centre is a one-stop clearinghouse for all information and resources pertaining to social business ideas and actions. Almost all the social business companies that we've created formulated their initial business concepts within Yunus Centre prior to establishing partnerships with other Grameen organizations. Yunus Centre monitors the progress of social businesses, facilitates and sustains relationships among social initiatives the world over, and fosters the spirit of the social business movement through events, social media, publications, and websites. It also organizes discussion groups to explore new frontiers of social business, conducts workshops and labs on the concept and practice of social business, and offers volunteer internships to young people from all over the world who want hands-on experience in social business that they can apply in their home countries.

The Grameen Creative Lab

The Grameen Creative Lab at Weisbaden (GCL) has become the engine for growth of global social business initiatives. It has assembled a very powerful and dedicated team to meet the ever-expanding demand for services needed in setting up world-class social businesses, particularly as joint ventures with leading companies. Based in the German city of Wiesbaden, near Frankfurt, GCL has set itself three main tasks: to communicate about social business; to incubate its own social businesses; and to support the creation of new social businesses by others. They call themselves an "action tank" (borrowing the phrase used by the American social entrepreneur Alan Khazei, founder of City Year): a center for combining the kind of study and analysis that a "think tank" does with the practical steps needed to turn concepts into realities.

GCL was created at the personal initiative of Hans Reitz, a self-made entrepreneur with that mixture of business drive and compassion that is so important to making our fight against poverty a success. Over the past three years, he has become a friend and adviser of mine. He jokingly calls our work "spreading the YY-virus" (named after Yunus). Among many other contributions, he helped me present the basic features of social business in the form of the seven principles we reviewed in Chapter 1.

I first met Reitz on a trip to Berlin in 2007. He introduced me to a number of key German business leaders, and I was impressed by his creativity. He was very interested in what we do and asked some probing questions. Soon after, he came to see us in Bangladesh for the first time, and we visited many of the Grameen companies together. Reitz was familiar with the problems of poverty—he has spent several years in rural India. With his unusual look (he has long hair and usually wears a broad-brimmed hat, scruffy clothes, and futuristic shoes), he was an interesting sight in our villages. Besides taking a closer look at Grameen through this visit, Reitz utilized the trip to produce a book about Grameen's diverse activities, *The Power of Dignity*, with moving pictures by photographer Roger Richter.

Reitz is a serial entrepreneur who has been involved in a number of businesses, including a forest-farming company in Kerala, India, a coffee chain in Germany, a creative communications agency (known as circ), and a corporate responsibility consultancy (circ responsibility). He also spent seven years studying the classical music of South India, so he is immersed in both the region's art and lifestyles.

I first appointed Reitz creative director of the Yunus Centre. Then, in 2008, we decided to set up the Grameen Creative Lab as a joint venture between circ responsibility and the Yunus Centre.

Recently, Reitz has decided to convert the circ responsibility itself into a social business. Next to Reitz, GCL is run by Saskia Bruysten, a charming and energetic former consultant for the Boston Consulting Group. GCL has gradually become the boiler room for all our social business projects outside Bangladesh. At the same time, the team of young, international people from various backgrounds working at GCL keeps on getting bigger and better.

As a social business, GCL pursues the cause of eradicating poverty while itself being economically sustainable. It took almost a year to become operationally sustainable, but by the latter half of 2009 it reached the break-even point. GCL accepts up to three months of volunteer services from interns who want to work there in order to learn about social business. Afterward, they can get paid staff appointments if they can identify clients or develop projects that allow GCL to expand and hire them as regular employees. GCL's operating costs are covered by such revenue-generating activities as consulting with large companies, governments, foundations, and other institutions or individuals on setting up social businesses and organizing seminars and other events for which attendance fees are charged.

Initially the consulting income was not easy to generate. Companies interested in setting up a social business saw their investment in the project as an act of generosity to be appreciated by Grameen, and they assumed that Grameen should come forward readily to provide all the solutions to their problems without any charge. They often did not see why they should pay a Grameen organization for advice and guidance. Over time, however, GCL managed to convince a number of companies that it makes good business sense to take advantage of its expertise—and that, like practically all valuable things, this expertise must be paid for if it is to be available to future beneficiaries. GCL bundles much of the experience and knowledge of existing social businesses, offers professional process support, and provides crucial creative impulses to developing social business ideas.

In its three chosen fields, GCL has already made huge strides. I myself am amazed at its dynamism. In terms of interacting and spreading the idea of social business, GCL works at several levels. It hosts regular Creative Labs in different countries where those who are interested in social business can meet to share their ideas and experiences. These workshops are very inspiring and educational for all the participants. GCL also offers intensive courses on the concept and practice of social business for business executives, students, foundations, governments official, academics, and other interested people. They are undertaking a series of workshops in Eastern European countries during the second half of 2010, which will bring knowledge of social business to a large and underserved portion of the world.

To spread the word about social business as widely as possible, GCL also creates large-scale events with the strong support of the event management team at circ. In November 2009, for instance, GCL hosted the first Global Grameen Meeting in Wolfsburg, Germany, where for the first time all the supporters, partners, and friends of social business came together. The event was timed to coincide with the twentieth anniversary of the fall of the Berlin Wall and to amplify our call for demolishing "the next wall to fall"—the wall of poverty. Every November hereafter there will be a Social Business Summit at which academics, students, entrepreneurs, social activists, investors, companies interested in starting social businesses, and all other interested persons will be welcome. In 2010, the summit will be hosted by Volkswagen at their center in Autostadt, Germany. In 2011, it will take place in Paris and be hosted by Crédit Agricole.

GCL has done excellent work in bringing the concept of social business to important business and civic leaders in Europe. For example, the mayor of the Italian city of Milan, Letizia Moratti, is working with GCL to highlight the powerful role that social business can play in our future economy. She is supporting our work with Unicredit to launch Grameen Italia, and also plans to highlight social business at Expo 2015, a "universal exposition" (similar to a world's fair) with the theme of "Feeding the Planet, Energy for Life," which will be hosted by Milan.

The main accomplishment of the GCL has so far been the support of large new social business undertakings, including joint ventures with BASF, the trading company Otto, and the sportswear company adidas. (I'll explain more about all these projects in the next chapter.) For some projects—namely those that take place in Bangladesh—Grameen is a potential joint-venture partner; in other cases, GCL transfers Grameen know-how into new social businesses independent of Grameen.

A social business can be set up by anyone, anywhere. The Yunus Centre and Grameen Creative Lab will consult with anyone who wants to set up a social business, spreading the concept in order to help eradicate poverty and solve the other economic and social problems that we see around us. (The GCL website, located at www.grameencl.com, includes a community page where interested people can link up online and expand their knowledge about, and involvement in, social business.) If a successful social business is like a seed, full of potential for growth, then the people of GCL are like so many Johnny Appleseeds, sowing orchards around the world that will soon be filled with delicious fruit.

University Centers for Exploring and Nurturing Social Business

Universities can play an important role in developing the future of social business. They are centers where enormous pools of expertise are located—knowledgeable professors and researchers who have studied and participated in practically every field you can imagine, from business and economics to healthcare, government, social services, engineering, information technology, and so on. Students are another valuable resource—young people filled with energy, idealism, and curiosity, many of whom are eager to explore new concepts in hopes of making a major impact on the world they will soon inherit. And universities are widely respected, nonpartisan civic institutions, giving them the ability to make fruitful connections among many kinds of organizations: government agencies, for-profit companies, charities, foundations, and citizens' groups. My own work leading to the creation of Grameen Bank occurred within a university environment while I was working as an economics professor at Chittagong University and was supported by my students, many of whom ultimately adopted Grameen Bank for building their lifelong careers.

Today a number of universities around the world are stepping up to act as catalysts and bridge-builders in the next phase of social business. An interesting example of the various ways academic institutions are promoting this cause can be seen in Scotland's Glasgow Caledonian University.

Glasgow is a historic city with a highly diverse population. It is also a city with significant social and economic problems. Often described as "postindustrial," Glasgow has suffered from the exodus of many companies that once provided livelihoods for thousands of families. And like many cities (for example, those in America's so-called Rust Belt states of the Upper Midwest), it is struggling to find its people new employment opportunities in twenty-first-century industries. These economic woes have had a significant social impact—for example, in the area of health. Glasgow suffers from some of the greatest wellness disparities in Europe. There are particular neighborhoods in the city where the average life expectancy for a male is over eighty, while in others it is stuck in the fifties.

I became aware of these problems after I was invited by Glasgow Caledonian University to receive an honorary degree. I could not go to Scotland to receive the degree for some time. Then finally, in November 2008, I went to receive the degree and give a public lecture. Vice-Chancellor Pamela Gillies went out of her way to make sure she utilized every moment of my stay at the university.

A series of fruitful meetings and conversations followed, and the result is a collection of initiatives that illustrate how a university can help spread and develop a new approach to society's ills.

First, the university decided to create the Grameen Caledonian Creative Lab, based in its Institute of Health and Wellbeing. The lab, which will officially begin its work in the spring of 2010, will house the new Yunus Centre for Social Business and Health, headed by a newly appointed Yunus Professor of Social Business, Cam Donaldson, a respected academic with an unusual and very appropriate background—he is an economist who formerly directed an institute for the study of health and society within the business school at the University of Newcastle in England. Thus, he can bring together perspectives from all these areas—health, economics, and business—in developing, implementing, and testing new social business ideas.

Second, the university invited Grameen Bank to collaborate with it in launching a microcredit organization named Grameen Scotland, to provide loans to help create self-employment, particularly among unemployed youth. Using Glasgow's run-down Sight Hill neighborhood as a laboratory, Grameen and the university will work together to create a program tailored to local needs and culture. One big challenge of the program will be to attract third-generation unemployed families into entrepreneurial activities supported through the credit program. The CEO of Grameen Trust, Professor H. I. Latifee, has already visited Glasgow and is preparing a set of detailed plans for the launch of this microcredit program in 2010.

What is exciting is that this new Grameen program will be the subject of a long-term, detailed study by researchers from the university (and perhaps from other institutions in Glasgow and elsewhere in Scotland) into the social and economic effect of microcredit. The special emphasis will be on health impacts. Over a period of ten years in the first instance, the researchers will examine such questions as: Do the families of Grameen borrowers have improved health conditions over time? Do they suffer from fewer disabilities, chronic conditions, and life-threatening illnesses? Is there an impact on life expectancies? Are infant mortality rates and serious childhood diseases affected? How do mental health indicators respond?

The hope is that this study, the first of its kind, will demonstrate a strong connection between public health and the availability of microcredit. If so, it will constitute a strong argument for including microcredit—and perhaps social business in general—in the list of tools to be deployed by governments and social service organizations that are trying to enhance the development prospects of countries, regions, and municipalities.

It's remarkable that this groundbreaking study will be taking place in Glasgow, the city where Adam Smith taught "moral philosophy" and wrote his epochal book on free markets, *The Wealth of Nations*. Perhaps this same city will now play a central role in advancing the next stage of development of the capitalist system—a stage I believe Smith, with his deep concern for the welfare of society and his trust in the power of "sympathy" among human beings to produce moral behaviors, would have understood and supported.

Finally, Glasgow Caledonian University is also partnering with Grameen on a social business project aimed at enhancing healthcare in Bangladesh. In early 2010, Professor Barbara Parfitt, former dean of the School of Nursing at the university, came to Bangladesh to spend about a year preparing to launch Grameen Caledonian Nursing College, which will train girls from the families of Grameen borrowers to become world-class nurses. Professor Parfitt has accepted the position of principal of the college. The college opened on March 1, 2010, with the first batch of close to forty students. All have received student loans from Grameen Bank to cover their expenses during their study period. As soon as they graduate from the college, they will have guaranteed jobs with Grameen Healthcare with a monthly salary of 15,000 taka (about $215), which is a very attractive salary for a new graduate. If they wish to work outside the country, Grameen Healthcare will help them find international jobs, and Grameen Bank will give them loans to pay their relocation costs. This will help make nursing an attractive profession for young girls in Grameen families. Instead of living a routine village life, these girls can become respected healthcare professionals and work both at home and abroad transforming themselves, their families, their villages.

As you can see, through Glasgow Caledonian University, the people of Bangladesh and the people of Scotland are about to enter into a multifaceted, two-way partnership—for the benefit of both. I believe that, in time, we will expand our partnership to include other forms of social business, with the university providing intellectual leadership and the research to validate the benefits being produced. The university's pro vice chancellor, Mike Smith, shares my excitement. "Our project with Grameen," he says, "has the potential to produce insights and approaches that may be significant not just for Glasgow or for Scotland but for all of Europe."

This program is just one of several university projects focused on social business in locations around the world.

The new California Institute of Social Business is based at the California State University's Channel Islands campus. It was created through the single-minded efforts of the university's president, Professor Richard R. Rush, who considers it a very important part of this new university. The ground was prepared through almost a year of intensive planning, including a series of lectures on microfinance and the development of ambitious curricula centered on social business for both the undergraduate college and the university's Martin V. Smith School of Business and Economics.

The Institute was finally launched in February 2010 with a flurry of activities. For the university's sixth annual Campus Reading Celebration, *Creating a World Without Poverty* was the chosen book, which meant that all 4,100 students and hundreds of faculty members shared the experience of reading and discussing it together. Then we held a grand opening celebration for the Institute, attended by some 1,500 local dignitaries and VIPs as well as many students and professors. The ceremony included my presentation of the first Yunus Social Innovation Medal to Steven M. Hilton, CEO and president of the Conrad N. Hilton Foundation, a well-known philanthropist.

Today the Institute is working on the further development of curriculum; detailing concepts and research opportunities in the social business arena; and studying the possibility of starting a social business venture fund to support emerging social businesses. Perhaps most exciting, it is developing an annual competition for social business plans, with the first contest to be held in September 2010. I'd love to see similar competitions become a regular feature of university business schools around the world.

With so much energy behind it, it seems clear that the California Institute of Social Business is poised to become a major center for social business innovation in the years to come.

On the other side of the Pacific, an equally exciting social business program with a very different focus is being developed. Under the leadership of Professor Masaharu Okada, an attorney with special expertise in intellectual property and high-tech entrepreneurship, Kyushu University in Fukuoka, Japan, has created a Grameen Technology Lab. Partnering with various Japanese companies, the lab will identify and develop uses of technology to alleviate social problems targeted by the Grameen family of companies. The new technologies will be jointly owned by the developing companies and the Grameen companies and then licensed to social businesses around the world.

Several projects are already under way at Kyushu University, including:

- One Village, One Portal—an experimental program for using high-tech information systems to collect and organize all kinds of social, economic, educational, agricultural, and cultural information about a particular village in Bangladesh, as a way of facilitating creative thinking and planning for sustainable solutions to social problems.
- E-Health and E-Agriculture projects for managing health records and agricultural information and making the data readily accessible by individuals and the institutes that serve them.
- An E-Passbook system that could be used by Grameen Bank borrowers for managing their savings, borrowing, and other financial services.

- Alternative power source experiments, testing new ways of generating, storing, transmitting, and using sustainable energy sources—solar, wind, biofuel, and so on.

Solutions devised by the students and faculty at Kyushu University will be applied first in Bangladesh, then adapted for use in other developing countries.

Yet another university program centered on social business is the Yunus Center at the Asian Institute of Technology in Bangkok, which is undertaking initiatives to understand and help to solve the problems of poverty through various forms of social business. Launched in August 2009, the Yunus Center at AIT will offer regular short courses on social business, microcredit, healthcare for the poor, environmental and gender equality issues, and other topics of importance for economic development.

The Yunus Center at AIT will also offer a special educational program to confer the title of Yunus Fellow of Social Business on a select group of highly-qualified students from a range of disciplines. We hope to attract various kinds of non-traditional candidates to this program, including homemakers, military officers, government officials, and others who will bring valuable life experience to the academic setting. To earn the title of Yunus Fellow, students will need to develop, plan, fund, and successfully implement a social business project in a community of their choice. Thus, a Yunus Fellow will be more than a scholar—he or she will also be an effective practitioner of social business with concrete achievements that benefit the poor.

Finally, HEC, the prestigious international business school located in Paris, has created a Social Business Chair, announced by President Sarkozy in April 2008. The first occupant of this position is Professor Frédéric Dalsace, a renowned scholar. The policy committee is co-chaired by me and Martin Hirsch, High Commissioner for Poverty Alleviation in Sarkozy's cabinet. Eleven professors from a range of disciplines devote part of their time to this program. They offer an ambitious 100-hour curriculum on social business and poverty reduc-tion that includes such challenging courses as "New Business Models at the Bottom of the Pyramid," "Business and Poverty in Developed Countries," and "Financing Social Business." The faculty attached to this program have begun working with various companies on social business projects. They say they will not be satisfied until they have ev-idence that HEC's "action tank" activities have contributed to a meas-urable decrease in poverty in France.

It's thrilling to me to see how social business has been embraced by some of the world's leading thinkers. The fact that universities in Asia, Europe, and North America are all involved in nurturing social business concepts can't help but accelerate the spread of social busi-ness to every corner of the globe.

I hope that, within the next few years, social business will become a standard part of the curriculum in every college, university, and grad-uate business school in the world. Students should be able to obtain an MBA degree with a concentration in social business, just as they now can focus on finance, marketing, or entrepreneurship. I predict that the universities that move first to add this component to their cur-riculum will attract many of the world's brightest and most idealistic students. Soon every university in the world will want to follow suit.

Social Investment Funds

To support the growth of social business, it will be important to cre-ate a number of investment funds committed to supporting social busi-nesses. Such funds will offer a number of services. They will study and evaluate fledgling social businesses, measuring their effectiveness in pursuing social goals and their financial and managerial efficiency, so that investment funds can be channeled to the most promising new ventures. They will serve as clearinghouses for information and ideas about social business, as their managers will quickly become some of the world's leading experts in what works, and what doesn't, in the social business arena. They will help to create a common vocabulary and set of measurement tools for defining success in social business, in much the way that such commonly agreed tools as ROE ("return on equity") and EBITDA ("earnings before interest, taxes, depreciations, and amortization") define financial success among profit-maximizing companies. They will make it easy for would-be social business investors to identify worthwhile companies to put their money into. And they will also provide a vehicle for instant diversification of social business investments: By writing a single check to a social investment fund, it should be possible to support dozens or even hundreds of social businesses that draw capital from that fund.

Some have raised the question how social business funds would pay for their own expenses, given the fact that the investments in social businesses cannot produce any dividends for investors. The solution is an annual management fee that the fund would be permitted to charge the companies receiving equity from the fund. The terms of this fee would need to be negotiated as part of the agreement between the fund and the social business. It's important that this fee be kept at a reasonable level (around 1 percent, for example), and funds may want to waive the fee until the companies they invest in reach the break-even point.

As I've already noted, there is a social business component fund within the Danone Communities Fund, which was launched in the spring of 2007 primarily as a vehicle to allow Danone shareholders, including Danone employees, to put a portion of their personal investment money into supporting the Grameen Danone yogurt company. It is underwritten and managed by Crédit Agricole, the largest retail bank in France and the second largest in Europe. In addition to managing the Danone Communities Fund, the bank has invested more than 50 million euros (around $70 million) to launch the Grameen Crédit Agricole Microfinance Foundation. This foundation is providing financing and other services in countries throughout the developing world, including Ethiopia, Mali, Kampuchea (formerly Cambodia), and Kosovo, and has earmarked a portion of its funds for investment in social business.

The Danone Communities Fund quickly became very popular, and with the influx of money from enthusiastic Danone shareholders came the opportunity—and the necessity—to identify other social businesses to receive funding.

Several other social business funds are already in the works. One is being developed in the principality of Monaco under the sponsorship of Prince Albert, that country's hereditary ruler. Known as the Yunus Monaco Fund, it will be a joint venture between the Yunus Centre and the Monaco Venture Capital and Private Equity Association. The initial funding target will probably be set around $100 million. Another fund is being planned in Germany. And the Islamic Development Bank (IDB) in Jeddah, Saudi Arabia, has announced plans to launch the IDB Grameen Social Business Initiative with an initial investment of more than $10 million.

The Next Step—A Social Stock Market

In the years to come, social business will continue to grow, gradually forming a parallel world alongside the familiar universe of profit-maximizing businesses. Social business companies will spring up in every country where free enterprise exists, and they will operate in almost every market and business arena, from consumer goods and services to corporate services, supplying, and outsourcing; and from finance and banking to information technology and heavy industry. Investment funds focused on social business will continue to multiply, and so will providers of services and products to help support this expanding universe—for example, investment management firms that specialize in social business, as well as information sources that concentrate on news and analysis about social business companies.

It seems inevitable that eventually a parallel stock market will spring up that is dedicated to raising investment capital for social businesses and to facilitating the buying and selling of social business shares. I first floated this idea in *Creating a World Without Poverty*. As I noted in that earlier book, it will be important to clearly define social business for the purpose of determining which companies are eligible to participate in the social stock market. Investors must have confidence that companies listed in the social stock market are truly social businesses, not profit-maximizing businesses or limited-profit-making companies claiming to be social businesses. The prices of shares on the social stock market will reflect the consensus of social investors as to the long-term value of the company whose ownership they represent. However, that value will be measured not in terms of profit expectations, but rather in terms of the social benefit produced, since that is the primary objective the social investor seeks.

As I envision it, there will be two different kinds of shares being traded in the social stock market: shares on which the original investment amount has already been repaid, and those where this is not the case. We might call the first category of shares "mature," on the analogy of bonds. When an investor buys a mature share in a social business, he or she cannot expect to receive any dividend from the company, because the original investment money has been fully repaid. However, a share that is not yet mature will carry with it the expectation of repayment, which of course will affect the share's value. Shares that are partially paid out will have their own demand and supply schedules. This is one reason we need a social stock market; it will facilitate discovery of the market price for shares in a given transaction.

Otherwise, the market will determine the price of both kinds of shares, and each category will have its own demand and supply curve. As in any market, sellers will seek to sell their shares at the best price they can get. At different prices, different numbers of shares will be sold. The higher the price, the larger the number of shares offered.

Under the principles of social business, the owner of a share is not supposed to accept any personal gain. Thus, if a sale of shares yields proceeds beyond the investment amount, the seller will be required to invest this money in another social business, invest in a social business fund, or buy a social business bond.

Why, then, should anybody sell his share in a social business? There are several probable reasons, including the following: to get back his investment money before the company can pay it back; to raise funds needed to buy shares of another social business; to invest in a social business fund; or to create his own private social business fund for future investment in social businesses.

On the other side, the buyer of a share would have his own reasons to buy it, such as social pride, emotional attachment, and desire to play a role in managing the company. He or she might also speculate in social business by investing in shares that appear to have a good chance of growing in value. The ultimate benefit would be the ability to sell those shares at a later date and thereby receive a larger sum that could be invested, in turn, in some other social business. Depending on the investor's sense of urgency or lack thereof, he or she will offer a relatively high or relatively low price. And as in any well-functioning market, the market price of the share will be decided on the day of trading based on that particular day's demand and supply.

Of course, the option of simply making a donation to a worthy cause is always available if the company is willing to accept a donation as a "non-recoverable investment." The donor/investor will be entitled to shares of the company, perhaps marked with some special designation to indicate the non-repayment status—Class B shares, for example. He or she can sell off these shares in the market and invest the sale proceeds in the same social business company or in another company, choosing either non-recoverable Class B shares or conventional repayable shares. Or an investor might choose to donate his shares to a social business fund (making the fund the owner of these shares) or, for that matter, to a charitable organization or foundation of his choice.

The price of a social business share will reflect the perceived effectiveness of the underlying company. If the social business demonstrates the ability to have a significant positive social impact, its share price will go up. As a result, investors' pride in their company will increase, and the stock will command a premium on the open market. Speculators who want to generate more money for their next social business venture will get active. The company will be enabled to expand its business, and incentives for new companies to enter into the same business will increase.

Whenever an investor buys a share in a social business, he or she helps to raise the price of the share by signaling to the company that its work is being appreciated by the public. As a result of this signal, such a company can easily expand its business by raising more money. At the same time, the investor has not "given away" his money. As a shareholder, he owns a piece of the company and can always resell his shares if he does not like the company's performance or if a more socially exciting company appears in the market. Thus, the existence of the social stock market provides valuable signals both to social businesses and to their investors as to the perceived effectiveness of companies in pursuing their social goals—signals that don't exist in the current universe of nonprofit or charitable organizations.

I hope someday soon the social stock market will come into existence. The number of social businesses issuing tradable stock will need to grow significantly before there is a need for a formal marketplace to facilitate such transactions. Under twenty-first-century conditions, there will probably be no need for the social stock market to have a physical location. Instead, it will be a virtual stock market in which all trading will take place electronically, as with today's NASDAQ exchange.

On the other hand, there might be a public relations value to opening one or more social stock market facilities in which investors, brokers, and traders could operate and which tourists and students could visit. Visitors could look down from balconies as social business specialists bought and sold shares on their computer screens; ever-changing share prices could scroll by on electronic display screens hanging overhead; and in a nearby hall, a series of exhibits covering the history of social business might be on display.

Eventually, the museum of poverty that I've often predicted might be located in an adjacent building. On a single excursion, young people could glimpse both the bygone problem of poverty and the story behind the mechanism that played a key role in its abolition—social business.

CHAPTER 8

Glimpses of Tomorrow

More Social Businesses
Are on the Way

As you've seen, the world of social business is a vibrant one. In the mere two years since the concept was first made public, it has attracted concrete interest from hundreds of directions. Individuals, corporations, foundations, non-profits, universities, think tanks, government agencies, and other organizations from every continent have contacted me and others at the Grameen family of businesses to learn more about social business and to ask how they can contribute. Within the space of this book, I cannot discuss all the initiatives currently under way or in the design stage—and by the time I finished writing it, it would already be out of date. For this reason, I've restricted myself to some of the most exciting projects taking shape and tried to use them to illustrate important lessons about the nature and potential of social business. I hope you've found these stories instructive and inspirational.

In this chapter, I am including some additional examples in abbreviated form, to demonstrate the variety of initiatives now emerging around the world. I'll also offer some further glimpses of the future of social business in some selected stories of other individuals, companies, and even governmental units that are creating the exciting social businesses of tomorrow.

Technology and Social Business:
The BASF Grameen Story

As I've stressed throughout this book, the business world has an incredible array of powerful technologies at its command—technologies that could revolutionize the lives of the poor. One example is BASF in Germany, which is one of the largest chemical companies in the world, deeply involved in industries ranging from plastics, construction, and agriculture to oil and gas production. It owns hundreds and hundreds of patents on chemical products, industrial processes, and other valuable techniques. And not all of these patents are currently creating wealth for BASF shareholders. Some BASF patents that are now dormant represent an amazing opportunity for the company to provide life-saving benefits to millions of the world's most disadvantaged people, and to do so in a way that will cost the owners of BASF little or nothing.

I know this is true because it was explained to me by no less an authority than the CEO of BASF himself. In one of our first discussions about the concept of social business, Dr. Jürgen Hambrecht told me, "We at BASF have thousands of patents lying around, just as many other industrial companies do. When we applied for these patents, each one had the potential to create an exciting business. But today, for various business reasons, many of them are practically useless to us. If you can use them to create social businesses that will help the poor, we'll be happy to let you take them."

Grameen and BASF are now working together on two social business projects. Both businesses, as it happens, are based on their patents which are in active commercial use. One is to manufacture and sell chemically treated mosquito-repellent netting in Bangladesh, making use of BASF's patented technology for producing such netting. The other is to produce and sell sachets containing micronutrients needed to improve the health of Bangladeshi children.

The need for mosquito netting in Bangladesh, as in many other developing nations, is based on a vital health concern. Malaria and other deadly diseases are spread predominantly through mosquito bites, which transmit infected blood from one individual to another. According to a 2009 report by the World Health Organization, 50.6 million people in Bangladesh are at risk of malaria, and 1.275 million cases of the disease were reported in 2008 alone.

Draining swamps, neglected ponds, and other sources of standing water that encourage the breeding of mosquitoes is an important long-term goal, but it's also a costly and difficult process. In the short term, the straightforward expedient of providing insect-proof coverings for the places where people sleep can dramatically reduce the incidence of these diseases. Yet tens of millions of people in Asia, Africa, and Latin America don't have access to this simple solution.

This is where BASF's patents come in. Manufactured under the brand name of Interceptor, the company's mosquito nets use Fendozin, a unique textile-finishing product that binds the insecticide Fendona in a special coating to the fibers of the net. Fendona is slowly released and rapidly kills or repels mosquitoes as they come into contact with the net. The net delivers this protection even after twenty washes. This means it has a useful life of three to four years, depending on local conditions.

On the nutritional side, BASF is a leading producer of dietary supplements that include the vitamins and trace elements needed to improve health, especially among children. The sachets BASF manufactures are designed to be incorporated into an individual's diet from one to three times per week. Earlier in this book, I described the serious problems with malnutrition from which millions of people, particularly women, suffer in Bangladesh. It's obvious how helpful these micronutrient supplements could be in addressing this challenge, and we plan to educate Bangladeshis about the benefits they can deliver.

The logical solution is to apply BASF's scientific know-how in the form of two businesses that will bring valuable solutions to the people who need them so desperately—and that is exactly what we are doing. Current plans call for BASF to provide start-up capital for these two businesses, both of which will be organized under the company label of BASF Grameen Ltd., a joint venture between BASF and the Grameen Healthcare Trust. The Agricultural Products division of BASF will supply a first batch of some 100,000 treated mosquito nets to be shipped from its producers in Thailand to distributors in Bangladesh. The initial supply of micronutrient sachets will be produced at BASF plants in Southeast Asia. As soon as a production unit is built in Bangladesh, production of the sachets will move there.

Sales and deliveries of both products in the countryside will be handled by local entrepreneurs, especially women, including both our familiar "Grameen ladies" and their grown-up daughters. Salespeople who need capital to start their operations will be able to obtain it from microloans via Grameen Bank. Thus, in addition to providing health benefits for users of the nets, this project will create business opportunities for people in rural Bangladesh. (We are constantly looking for these sorts of double opportunities when developing social businesses.)

As you might expect from a highly successful global corporation, BASF has developed a detailed and thorough business plan for this joint venture. According to current estimates, BASF Grameen will begin producing the mosquito nets during 2010. It should break even financially in 2011, and the repayment to BASF of the start-up investment will begin in 2015. By 2013, annual sales of Interceptor nets should exceed 200,000, while sales of micronutrient sachets will pass 10 million per year. The benefits for the people of Bangladesh will be enormous.

Digital Solutions for the World's Poor: Grameen Intel Projects

Another leading company with a wealth of amazing technology at its disposal is Intel. When Craig Barrett, then the chairman of Intel, expressed interest in launching a social business using some of Intel's information technology to benefit poor people during a visit to Dhaka in September 2007, I quickly agreed.

Grameen Intel is designed as a social business that is "entrepreneurial, sustainable, and a benefit to the local community." Grameen Intel is now building up an IT-based healthcare service for the poor in Bangladesh through a pilot project that concentrates on infant-maternal health.

This is a serious issue in Bangladesh, just as it is in countries throughout the developing world. Every year, over 120,000 infants die needlessly in Bangladesh, many due to nutritional deficiencies—anemia, shortages of vitamins and minerals, and other problems that should be remediable. In addition, around 12,000 mothers die from pregnancy-related complications. These numbers are obviously unacceptable, and in the Grameen organizations' focus on healthcare they have received significant attention.

Of course, fixing these problems is not easy. In particular, bringing improved healthcare to babies and mothers in rural villages before, during, and after pregnancy is very challenging. Traveling great distances over poorly maintained roads is difficult for doctors and nurses; enticing physicians and other professionals to live and work in the impoverished countryside rather than in one of the large cities of Bangladesh is very challenging; and the country as a whole has a serious shortage of nurses, in particular.

The Grameen-Intel pilot program, which was launched in the summer of 2009, is designed to test whether IT technology can play a significant role in improving the dismal statistics associated with infant-maternal health. Can electronic methods of data gathering and communication help fill the gap between the pregnant mother in the remote village and the experienced physicians many miles away? This is what Grameen Intel hopes to determine.

The pilot project is based in two villages in Savar, a semi-rural area on the outskirts of the capital city of Dhaka. The technology solution being tested uses smart phones with special software designed by the Grameen Intel team for measuring the risk level of a woman's pregnancy.

Armed with these smart phones, mobile healthcare workers hired and trained by Grameen Intel have been traveling from door to door in the villages, visiting with pregnant mothers and administering twenty-item questionnaires designed to separate moderate-risk from high-risk pregnancies. This is like the prescreening that patients in a country like the United States might receive from a highly trained nurse prior to visiting the doctor. In our program, the role of the professional nurse is played by healthcare workers assisted by powerful technology. Two physicians, who can be located anywhere, then survey the data, identifying potential dangers to the infants and mothers.

The results so far have underscored the seriousness of the problem. Out of the first ninety-two mothers surveyed, forty-eight were rated as high-risk. These mothers need to visit a clinic for further diagnosis and care. The next step, of course, will be to develop a program through our healthcare company, Grameen Kalyan, to make the connection to follow-up care. This, too, will be part of the Grameen Intel pilot project. Information is the vital first step, but it's not enough—action to really improve infant-maternal health must also be part of the equation. The project is planned to expand from two clinics to ten during 2010, while simultaneously working to improve the provision of follow-up care to mothers who need it.

The ultimate goal is an IT-based product/service combination that can be used by a local entrepreneur to provide a social benefit to the people of Bangladesh. Grameen Intel now envisions two groups of people from whom these entrepreneurs could be drawn. One is "Grameen ladies"—women who are borrowers from Grameen Bank, many of whom are looking for new business opportunities. They are deeply connected to the communities where they live, and they can use those social connections to find customers for the new IT-based businesses Grameen Intel will foster.

The other group is what we call Grameen's New Entrepreneurs (GNEs). These are children of Grameen borrowers who have gone through higher education with help from student loans provided by Grameen Bank. Many of these GNEs are already working in enterprises launched through the Grameen family of companies—for example, Grameen Shakti, our renewable-energy company, employs many young people trained as engineers to build, install, and maintain solar panels and biogas systems in local communities around Bangladesh. Once the Grameen Intel program is in full swing, many of these GNEs could become IT entrepreneurs.

It's interesting to note that more than 1,500 students in Bangladesh today are enrolled in medical schools and engineering programs. They come from poor and illiterate families in villages that are struggling economically. This means that, even after they earn their degrees, they may find it difficult to get jobs. Opening up the opportunity to create a livelihood by becoming an IT entrepreneur can make a huge difference, not only for these smart and motivated individuals but for their entire families.

Thus, the Grameen Intel social business should, over time, spawn many more small-scale local businesses that will enable thousands of people to work their way out of poverty. In this sense, the comparison to the Grameen phone ladies is an appropriate one: In both cases, new technology tools are providing poor people with a way to start a socially useful business that will both spur growth in the local economy and provide income to the entrepreneur.

Other Health-Related Social Business Collaborations

Both the BASF and Intel joint ventures are focused on healthcare issues, which are crucially important in Bangladesh just as they are throughout the developing nations. I want to briefly mention several other health-related social business projects that are currently under development. Each has the potential to bring enormous health benefits to the people of Bangladesh.

- Grameen and Pfizer, the famous pharmaceutical and healthcare corporation, are collaborating on a project to evaluate and improve the delivery of care through village clinics by Grameen

Healthcare. The focus of the first pilot program will be maternal-child health, which we consider the single most important issue for low-income families in Bangladesh.

- GE Healthcare, a major supplier of medical technology and services, is working with Grameen Healthcare to develop improved care delivery systems for our primary care clinics in Bangladesh, with special emphasis on pregnancy care. Among other elements, this project is entrusted with the task of designing inexpensive portable ultrasound equipment capable of working in rural areas to deliver this service in patients' homes. After GE designers and engineers spent months in Bangladesh working on this project, they demonstrated the first model in March 2010—a very impressive presentation. The device has already been field-tested by healthcare workers trained in its operation. GE Healthcare also demonstrated a new highly compact ultra-sound device that produces color images and can actually hang from a doctor's neck like a stethoscope. We are going to develop a social business model that will let young women in the villages become high-tech diagnosticians, helping to save the lives of pregnant mothers and their children.

- Johnson & Johnson, the pharmaceuticals company, is working with Grameen to develop effective protocols for running mother-child health care centers in the village as well as training our doctors and paramedics to improve their efficiency. The systems and models they develop will be replicated in many locations, bringing benefits to thousands of patients.

- The Mayo Clinic, one of the world's leading centers of medical knowledge and practice, is collaborating with Grameen Healthcare on a project to improve the prevention, diagnosis, and treatment of parasitic diseases, a common problem in the developing world. Insights from this project into more effective low-cost methods of delivering services to the poor may eventually be applied by the Mayo Clinic to help treat underserved populations in the United States.

- You might not think of a clothing company as being involved in healthcare, but the Japanese firm of UNIQLO plans to approach the manufacture of clothing in Bangladesh as a social business with a focus on health benefits. Having visited the villages and studied conditions there, UNIQLO believes that making its unique Heat-Tech and fleece garments available at minimal cost will protect poor people against bad weather conditions and reduce the spread of malaria and other infectious diseases.

New social business projects related to healthcare are coming on line all the time. In another year or two I may have to write a whole new book just to describe them all!

Social Business Type II: Otto Grameen

Grameen Bank shows that it is possible for a social business to provide social benefits in two ways at once—by creating products or services that help solve a social problem *and* by providing income for its owners, who are poor. The loans the bank disburses provide capital that allows poor people to start or expand businesses and so work their way out of poverty. At the same time, because the bank is owned by the poor, it benefits them through having a real voice in managing the bank and, of course, through the annual dividend checks they receive.

These two kinds of benefits reflect the two kinds of social businesses. Type I is a business that provides goods or services to advance a social goal while being owned by people who are not themselves poor or underpriviledged. It generates no profits or dividends for its owners; any surplus is reinvested to finance the growth of the business and to expand the benefits it provides to society. Most of the social businesses

I've discussed in this book, including Grameen Danone, Grameen Veolia Water, BASF Grameen, and Grameen Intel have been of this type.

A Type II social business is either actually owned by poor people (as is the case with Grameen Bank), or owned by a specially-created trust to deliver benefits to the poor. A social business owned by the poor benefits the poor by generating income for them directly. However, since individual ownership leads to complicated legal issues under the present legal system, one way to bring all the benefits of a for-profit company to the poor or specific disadvantaged groups is to give the ownership to a trust which transfers these benefits to the intended group of people.

In this variation of Type II social business, the effectiveness of the organization and its ability to bring social benefits to the poor will depend heavily on the talent and integrity of the board members who administer the trust. It will be essential for the trust to choose the right people for its board and for the trust to operate with full transparency. In time, as the infrastructure of social business grows to include a social stock market with many active investors, share rating agencies, and numerous social business investment funds, these organizations will provide additional scrutiny to make sure that the trusts manage Type II social businesses with a high level of integrity and skill.

Other than Grameen Bank, there have been no other examples of Type II social businesses—until now. We are now working with the German company Otto to create a Type II social business. It will be called the Otto Grameen Textile Company.

Otto GmbH is a mail order and trading company that deals in textiles as well as other products. It has an important role in shaping markets because it helps define production standards for many of the goods it trades. Aid by Trade—founded by Dr. Michael Otto, owner of Otto GmbH—is deeply involved in creating a sustainable cotton industry for Africa. In this role, Dr. Otto has done a lot to support the concept of sustainability.

The concept for Otto Grameen began to take shape during a meeting in February 2009 that included me, Saskia Bruysten (the director of Grameen Creative Lab), and Dr. Otto. Otto was very interested in helping to start a social business in partnership with Grameen—but what kind of business should it be? In subsequent meetings, the idea of a textile business that would be owned by a trust dedicated to helping the poor—that is, a Type II social business—first surfaced. After some discussion and exploration of the implications, Otto agreed to the concept in a subsequent meeting in April.

The development of the project concept has proceeded under the direction of Hassan Ashraf, who is very knowledgeable about the textile industry in Bangladesh, having served as CEO of Grameen Knitwear. Ashraf and the leaders of Otto are working on ideas for a product line and a marketing plan. Initially at least, they don't expect to produce garments or textiles to be marketed under the Otto Grameen brand name; instead, they will manufacture goods that customer companies can market under their own brand names. But this approach could change over time as Otto Grameen develops experience and a reputation, and as market conditions evolve. (Like any business, Otto Grameen will be continuously on the lookout for exciting market opportunities that it can take advantage of to support its core mission: to generate profits and benefits for the poor.)

According to the current legal structure, Otto Grameen is owned by an entity named Otto Grameen Trust whose dedicated purpose is to utilize its income for the benefit of a defined group of poor people that will include the company workers, their families, and the communities in which the company operates. Otto Grameen Trust has set up a for-profit company called Otto Grameen Textile Company as a joint venture between the Otto Group (owning 90 percent shares) and Grameen Trust (10 percent). Profits of the textile company will go to Otto Grameen Trust, which will ensure that the income and equity growth generated by Otto Grameen is spent as intended—to benefit the poor.

Otto will provide OGT with two no-interest loans, which will serve as seed money. The first loan will be used as capital for launching the business, the second to fund an endowment for the social services the company will provide. The idea is to start offering these social services as quickly as possible rather than to wait until the company is throwing off profits to fund the services. Otto will also contribute technical knowledge and its market-making expertise; Grameen Trust will provide its knowledge of local conditions, culture, and social issues.

According to the nonbinding memorandum of understanding that Otto and Grameen Trust have signed, the goal is to establish a factory to produce clothing for the export market, manufacturing between 200,000 and 250,000 garments per month and employing between two hundred and five hundred workers. "Dignified working conditions, social services and income and ownership prospects" are to be afforded all the workers, and emphasis will be placed on hiring "disadvantaged" workers, including women, single parents, and the illiterate.

The plant will also be ecologically and economically sustainable. The team in charge of detailed planning is currently engaged in research into optimal choices for building materials, energy consumption, and supply chain management. Helping from the Otto side is a company subsidiary known as Systain, which focuses on sustainable energy projects.

Solar panels will be used to contribute as much of the factory's energy needs as possible, supplemented as necessary by a gas generator or other conventional source. Common local building methods, including the use of highly insulating mud bricks and bamboo rods for framing, will be adapted as far as possible. The siting, orientation, and design of the factory will be carefully planned to take maximum advantage of natural forces in cooling and heating the facility (for example, by positioning windows to allow cross-ventilation while allowing minimal heat absorption during periods of intense summer sunlight).

Options for shipping raw materials and finished products that maximize efficiency and minimize carbon emissions are also being explored. The hope is to operate a truly carbon-neutral factory that can serve as a model for similar facilities throughout Bangladesh and the rest of South Asia.

The profits the business generates will be disbursed into three channels. A portion will go to repay the no-interest loans provided by Otto. (The current estimate is that this repayment process will take at least ten years.) Another share will be set aside as an operating reserve for the company in case of economic difficulties and as a fund for eventual expansion. But the most important share—and the one that will be allocated first when the books are balanced every month—will go to providing social services to the poor people who are designated as the main beneficiaries of Otto Grameen.

In addition to decent wages and normal employment benefits, the social benefits to be offered by Otto Grameen are slated to include:

- Access to healthy, nutritious food
- Healthcare
- Educational assistance and worker training
- Access to credit
- Assistance with housing
- Individual or virtual ownership prospects for the company's workers

Initially these social benefits will be provided to Otto Grameen workers and their families. In time they may be expanded to include others in the community. Ultimately it is possible that each Otto Grameen factory might anchor a "Otto Grameen village" in which everyone enjoys a higher standard of living thanks to the company's presence in the community.

As you can see, the plans for Otto Grameen are quite ambitious. It's an exciting project with many features that are unprecedented. Undoubtedly the Otto Grameen team will find it necessary to make adjustments and changes along the way as they discover what works and what doesn't, and as they develop new solutions to unexpected problems that may arise. Current plans call for construction of the first factory during 2010, with an estimated budget somewhere between 1 and 2 million euros (roughly $1.2 million to $2.8 million), depending on a number of factors, such as the feasibility and cost of solar energy systems and sustainable building materials, that haven't yet been determined. The start of production is tentatively scheduled for the first quarter of 2011.

If Otto Grameen can make this experiment successful, it will provide a model to many future enterprises along the same lines.

Shoes for All: The Grameen Adidas Quest

The companies of the adidas Group include adidas brand, Reebok, Rockport, and TaylorMade Golf. The adidas Group strives to be the global leader in the sporting goods industry. The company competes in this lucrative, high-visibility marketplace by marshalling the star power of fashion designers, professional athletes, and celebrities.

It's easy to think of this industry as one centered on glamour, leisure, and entertainment, with little direct relevance to the needs of poor people. I used to think of it that way, and I never thought that Grameen or I would have anything to do with adidas. But strange circumstances brought us together. While visiting Germany in November 2008, I was invited to have a talk with adidas Group CEO Herbert Hainer. He wanted to understand the concept of social business. In a meeting at the group's headquarters, I tried to explain the idea as best as I could.

Then the question naturally arose, what could adidas do in the way of social business? I had no idea what I should suggest. Finally, I said, "Maybe adidas can start with a statement of commitment, something like this: Nobody in the world should go without shoes. As a shoe company, it is our responsibility to make shoes affordable even to the poorest person."

I asked Hainer whether a statement like this made sense to him. "It does," he said. "But I am trying to understand its full implications. Can we take a break for a while? My colleagues will give you a guided tour of our headquarters and its fascinating museum while I consult with my senior colleagues about our discussion."

We met again at lunch time. Hainer's senior colleagues also joined the lunch. As we ate together, Herbert quietly asked me how cheap shoes would have to be to make them affordable to the poorest. I readily responded, "Maybe under one dollar or so, I guess."

Hainer stopped eating for a few moments while keeping his eyes fixed on me. I thought this was the end of our discussion on social business. But when lunch was finished, Hainer surprised me. He wanted to make an announcement. He declared that the adidas Group would join Grameen in launching a social business to produce shoes for the poor in Bangladesh. These shoes should be sold at a price as close as possible to one euro—not exactly the same as a dollar, but very close. I couldn't believe I was hearing such a bold pronouncement from the CEO!

His top executives immediately sat down with me in a business session to work out a plan of action. Suddenly they were all seized by an enormous amount of energy and enthusiasm. I was listening to their plans, answering a flood of questions, and marveling at the power social business has to transform people so quickly!

Herbert Hainer put together a team of eight "high-potential" adidas managers from various company departments—marketing, finance, and business development—to study possible social business projects. They have been visiting villages of Bangladesh, meeting poor men, women, and children, and studying their preferences, needs, consumption priorities, disposable income, expenditure patterns, and so on.

They realized very quickly that providing shoes for the poor in Bangladesh is not just a comfort issue, it is a major health need. We forget that shoes are, in fact, intimately connected with human health.

Parasitic diseases attack the human body through the skin of the feet. Diseases like hookworm are widespread in Bangladesh because millions of people go barefoot. Children are the most vulnerable group for this disease.

Following an internal project review, the Reebok Brand began creating a plan to move forward with the next phase of the project. The project represented a remarkable challenge that Reebok would have to accept: to design and market footwear that is affordable by practically everyone on this planet. While the results of the initial study outlined some issues that may prove rather difficult to overcome, they are not giving up. Reebok is pushing forward, aiming to create a shoe that is not only extremely affordable but also recyclable and desirable in the eyes of customers. This last requirement is one that many companies might have eliminated when trying to launch a shoe company as a social business. After all, if this is a "do-good" project, why bother with esthetic appeal? Won't the poor people be grateful to have any kind of shoes at all, even if they are ugly?

That is the wrong spirit to apply to the project. Social business is about joy!—not about people compelled by their circumstances to settle for second-best. Those who will wear these shoes should be proud of them. It should bring them respect and dignity, not just protection. Reebok wants to create affordable shoes that will be positively cool— that the poor people of rural Africa, South Asia, and Latin America will regard as a mark of good taste and respectability.

And being cool isn't just something that would be nice to achieve— it has important practical benefits. The greater the demand for the shoes, the bigger the production volumes—and the lower the price can be. So Reebok is applying its best design, fashion, and marketing thinking to the one-euro-shoe project, and it plans to crack that price barrier in style.

Under current plans, 15,000 pairs of newly-produced shoes from Reebok will arrive in Bangladesh by August 2010 for test marketing. We'll learn about the users' reactions, their preferences, how demand varies by age and gender, and so on. Then Reebok will further refine the product and business model for the project's next phase.

Creating Jobs: Grameen Employment Services

Migrant workers from Bangladesh—and from elsewhere in South Asia—are often badly exploited. Desperate for work, they travel far from home to provide labor wherever the need is greatest, living in barracks or other temporary shelters and sending money back home to support their hungry families. Under these circumstances, they are vulnerable to serious abuse. Standards of fair pay, decent working conditions, livable housing, and healthcare are often nonexistent or difficult to enforce. When companies run into financial difficulties or go bankrupt, migrant employees may go unpaid or suddenly find themselves jobless and without even a plane ticket to return home. (This was the fate of thousands of Bangladeshi construction workers when the economic crash of 2008–2009 brought a sudden halt to the building boom in the Middle East.)

To relieve the plight of these workers, we are developing a social business to be called Grameen Employment Services (GES). Like conventional employment agencies, GES will serve as a subcontractor to large companies looking for a reliable source of competent workers. However, as a social business, GES will pursue policies designed to protect employees and help them enhance their value on the labor market. It will provide language training (so that migrant workers will be better able to contribute effectively on the job—as well as to speak up in defense of their own interests) as well as basic skills training and such services as help with arranging passports, visas, and medical tests. It will also represent the interests of workers in their dealings with employers—for example, by making sure that housing and safety conditions are adequate and by guaranteeing that workers receive every penny of pay that is due them.

Remittances from Bangladeshis working abroad make a significant contribution to the country's economy, as is the case in many parts of the developing world. GES will help keep this vital source of money flowing to the families and villages that depend on it while also protecting the human dignity of the workers whose labor creates it.

Using Social Business to Rejuvenate Regional Economies: Projects in Colombia, Albania, and Haiti

One of the most challenging—and potentially exciting—areas for social business will be working to revitalize entire economies that are struggling under the burdens of poverty. The potential exists to bring together resources from many players—government agencies, NGOs, private companies, and individual citizens—to create powerful poverty-alleviating programs centered on the propulsive force of social business. The first ambitious project along these lines will be launched in June 2010 in Caldas, Colombia, and by the time you read these words there will be others under way.

Caldas is an economically underdeveloped province in the Paisa region of Colombia. While Caldas was once one of the country's biggest coffee producers, it has since been experiencing a depression due to the collapse of the coffee market in the area, causing a sharp increase in unemployment. In Caldas today, about 62 percent of the population lives on less than $2 per day, while fully one-quarter lives on less than $1 per day—the benchmarks commonly used for measuring poverty and extreme poverty, respectively. Colombia itself is a very troubled country economically, ranking seventy-seventh on global development lists, having the sixth-greatest level of income inequality in the world, and suffering from the second-highest number of displaced persons (thanks to ongoing wars among cocaine cartels and oppression by local militia groups).

In mid-2009, while I was attending the Regional Microcredit Summit for Latin America and the Caribbean, in Cartagena, Mr. Aristizábal Muñoz, the governor of Caldas province, came to ask whether I could help him restart his region's economy. While listening to him describe the area's problems, I had an idea—why not start a series of social businesses to address these troubles?

I gave Muñoz an outline of what I was willing to do if he liked the ideas and agreed to support them with funding. I told him, "I'll create a fund to be called the Social Business Fund of Caldas, as well as a Social Business Trust which will set up and own social businesses in the province. These social businesses will create employment, provide microcredit, and offer services like healthcare, insurance, the marketing of agricultural goods, and so on. I think we can launch these efforts if you can provide a seed fund of around sixteen million U.S. dollars." Muñoz listened carefully and agreed in principle.

Later I followed up on this proposal. Governor Muñoz invited our project preparation team, headed by Hans Reitz from Grameen Creative Lab in Weisbaden, to visit his people in Caldas. We worked hard to refine our thinking about the project. And on November 7, 2009, at the Grameen Social Business Conference in Wolfsburg, Germany, a memorandum of understanding was signed between me and Muñoz to implement microfinance and social business projects in the department. Caldas is planning to invest $16 million as a start-up fund for the microcredit and social business program.

The social business programs in Caldas will include both Type I businesses and Type II businesses owned by trusts that will administer the profits for the benefit of local people.

As part of this program, we are recruiting young Colombians who are now working in North America and Europe to go back home and work in the social businesses we are creating in Caldas. This will be a challenge that they may find worth accepting. If they do, it will bring another benefit to Colombia by attracting more of the country's brightest young people to remain in the country and work to build its future.

A similar program is now in the planning stage with the government of Albania, one of the most economically-troubled countries in Europe. Sali Berisha, the prime minister of Albania, met me in New York in October 2009 and described the terrible situation of the poor in his country. He promised to support any poverty-reducing programs that I would like to launch in Albania. Immediately recalling my conversation with Governor Muñoz of Caldas, I proposed a similar program to Mr. Berisha, and he agreed immediately.

I sent Reitz and his team to explain the social business concept to governmental and business leaders in Albania, just as they had done in Caldas. Soon GCL had developed a detailed proposal for what it dubs a Holistic Social Business Initiative that can help jump-start economic growth in the country. The proposal was presented on January 22, 2010, in a meeting in Tirana attended by the prime minister as well as leaders from the business world, academia, civil society, NGOs, the microfinance sector, and government. We expect the program to be formally launched by the second half of 2010.

A third such project is also being developed in Haiti as part of the rebuilding effort being launched in the wake of the devastating earthquake that struck the island nation in January 2010.

Like millions of others, I watch the tremendous outpouring of sympathy and support for the earthquake victims from governments, companies, foundations, and individuals around the world. At the annual Davos meeting, also in January 2010, I mentioned to Léo Apotheker, the co-CEO of SAP, my concern that this large amount of financial help generated for Haiti might not be utilized properly because of its exclusive focus on immediate relief rather than mid-term and long-term development. "Maybe we should create a Social Business Fund for Haiti," I said, "to which 10 percent or more of all the relief money could go."

Apotheker immediately responded, "We are sending a large amount of money ourselves. Maybe we should put our money in this Social Business Fund."

I said, "Why not? Let's do it."

After I announced creation of the fund later that week, many people and companies have responded favorably. We plan to start a series of social businesses in Haiti in fields such as housing, healthcare, agriculture, forestry, job creation, microfinance, marketing, training, employment, and so on. We'll also create a Social Business Trust of Haiti that will help businesses from around the world to come to Haiti to create social businesses of their own. We already have an office on the ground to organize the Haiti initiative, and a team led by Hans Reitz is detailing our plan of action.

All three of these country initiatives address a new challenge for social business. They represent an important test of the power of social business to help jump-start an economic development process focused on the poor at a national or sub-national level. The results should be fascinating to watch and potentially very significant for other economies around the world. If these projects meet our expectations, it seems likely that social business may become a major tool for policy-makers and others who are looking for ways to accelerate the pace of economic development in countries around the world.

CHAPTER 9

The End of Poverty

The Time Is Here

Since the end of the Second World War, we have witnessed the triumphal advance of the capitalistic system. The economies of North America, Europe, and Japan prospered to an unprecedented extent, and millions of individuals became extremely wealthy. But at the same time, billions of people around the world were left behind.

Determined to reduce the tragic gap between the Global North and the Global South, the peoples of the world came together at the United Nations in New York in 2000. They agreed on eight important goals they wanted to achieve by 2015—the so-called Millennium Development Goals. The most important of these was to cut the rate of poverty in half.

Bangladesh is one country that has made tremendous progress toward achieving the Millennium Goals. Its poverty rate has fallen from an estimated 57 percent in 1991 to 40 percent in 2005. Though still too high, it continues to fall by around 2 percent a year, with each percentage point representing a meaningful improvement in the lives of millions of Bangladeshis. The country is on track to achieve the goal of reducing poverty by half in 2015. Even more remarkable, Bangladesh's rapid economic growth has been accompanied by little increase in internal inequality (as revealed by such statistical indicators as the Gini coefficient, a measure of "statistical dispersion" commonly used to define degrees of inequality within a given population).

For a number of years, many other countries in Asia showed similar success to Bangladesh. In general, in many countries around the world, things slowly started to improve. The number of people who live on less than $1.25 per day decreased from an estimated 1.8 billion to 1.4 billion from 1990 to 2005—though this still represented some 25 percent of the world's population.

But since then, the little blaze of hope lit by the Millennium proclamation has been extinguished by a complex global crisis—economic, financial, environmental, agricultural, and social. Recent estimates suggest that some 55 million to 90 million people have been added to the extreme-poverty rolls, all due to a global crisis that was certainly not of their making.

This crisis first hit us in 2008 in the form of a food crisis. Food prices, especially those of staples such as corn and rice, became unaffordable for poor people all over the world. Wheat alone has risen in price by 200 percent since the year 2000. This is causing enormous hardship and even starvation for additional millions of people.

The causes for that tragic development were various. On the one hand, the constant growth of the world's population accompanied by a decline of the total amount of arable land was responsible for escalating food prices. In addition, millions of people who are coming out of poverty and many more who are improving their economic condition are consuming more food than before. At the same time, distorted global markets raised prices, and even destroyed national and regional agricultural systems that once boasted enormous food surpluses.

Subsidies for ethanol in countries like the United States are one example of this problem. Intended to encourage the growth of corn and soy to partially replace fossil fuels in gasoline, they made it economically viable to use biofuels as a partial substitute for oil. But these kinds of subsidies led to unintended ecological, social, and economic consequences, including upward pressure on the price of basic food-stuffs thanks to the diversion of farmland and other agricultural resources to the production of fuel rather than food. In the interest of global food security, it is obvious that such subsidies should be withdrawn as quickly as possible.

In addition, speculators drove up the prices for raw materials. I'm referring to big investors, mostly in the developed world, who used futures markets in wheat, corn, soybeans, and other commodities merely as trading tokens. These speculators did not have a real interest in the raw materials they traded and never intended to actually use them. Instead, they bought and sold contracts in these commodities simply to realize monetary profits. Thanks to today's electronic trading systems, modern financial markets allowed speculators to trade unbelievably large amounts of raw materials within seconds with just a few clicks on their computers. The speculators may have profited from these deals, but people whose lives depended on access to the underlying commodities suffered.

It's a tragic, yet obvious, illustration of how our economic system fails in its mission to serve the needs of *all* humanity. Millions of people around the world are suffering because a few speculators blindly grasp at profits.

All of these economic problems are growing worse just as global environmental trends threaten the future of agriculture around the world. Climate change, drought, and deforestation are turning vast areas that were once fertile farmlands into deserts. The UN reports that every year an area equivalent to the entire country of Ukraine is lost to farming because of climate change. What's more, if current global warming trends continue, over the next century, rising sea levels can be expected to flood almost one-third of the world's farmland. It is easy to imagine what will happen to Bangladesh, the world's most densely populated country, which is a flat country with 20 percent of its land less than three feet above sea level. It is an emerging case of environmental disaster immediately turning into human disaster.

But it is not just the food crisis and the environmental crisis that have worsened conditions for the world's poor people. The financial crisis has also done terrible damage. When credit markets seize up, when banks stop lending, when businesses by the thousand fail, and when government aid programs collapse due to falling revenues, it is the poor who suffer most.

The financial crisis has shown us more clearly than ever where capitalism fails. Originally the credit market was designed to serve people's needs. It was designed to provide businessmen with capital to found or expand companies. Thanks to home mortgages, people were able to buy homes and pay the costs over a long period of time. Student loans funded education for millions. Banks that provided the credit earned a reasonable profit. Everyone benefited.

But traditional capitalism demands ever-increasing profits, and it creates powerful incentives for smart people to use their creativity to make that possible. Over time, competing financial institutions aimed for higher and higher profits in the credit market using clever feats of financial engineering. They repackaged mortgages and other loans into sophisticated instruments whose risk level and other characteristics were hidden or disguised. Then they sold and resold these instruments, earning a slice of profit on every transaction. All the while, investors eagerly bid up the prices, scrambling for unsustainable growth. Blinded by these unrealistically high rates of return, they never made an effort to question the risks hidden inside those financial instruments. They gambled that the system's underlying weakness would never come to light.

But it did. With the collapse of the housing market in the United States, the whole house of cards tumbled down with such momentum it surprised even those of us who had been skeptical about the financial system all along. Millions of people around the world who did nothing wrong are suffering. As always, the ones who are hit the hardest are the poor—especially the "bottom 3 billion," who were already living at a bare subsistence level. They are being hit hard by the combined effects of the food crisis, the environmental crisis, and the financial crisis. In its current, incomplete form, capitalism has badly failed its social responsibility.

However, as wise people throughout history have known, a great crisis offers great opportunity. Sadly, the world is not yet paying attention to this aspect of the crisis.

So far, governments struggling to alleviate the combined crises of 2008–2010 have kept themselves busy coming up with super-sized bail-out packages for the institutions responsible for creating the financial crisis. Unfortunately, no bail-out package of any size has even been discussed for the victims of the crisis: the bottom 3 billion and the planet itself.

Today's crisis has been a valuable reminder that all people around the world are undeniably connected. The fate of Lehman Brothers and that of the poor women working in a garment factory in Bangladesh are linked. Therefore, I have repeatedly urged that this mega-crisis be taken as an opportunity to redesign the existing economic and financial systems. This is the time to bring the world together and to change our economic architecture so that this type of crisis never occurs again. Social business can be a key element of this change.

The most important feature of this new global economic architecture will be to complete the half-built theoretical framework of capitalism by including a second type of business, social business, in the global marketplace. Once social business becomes a recognized element in the framework, it can play a very important role in solving the financial crisis, the food crisis, and the environmental crisis. Furthermore, it can provide the most effective institutional mechanism for resolving poverty, homelessness, hunger, and ill health. Social business can address all the problems left behind by the profit-making businesses and at the same time can reduce the excesses of the profit-making businesses.

The new economic architecture I propose would not turn back the clock on globalization. It will support and enhance globalization by making sure that it works for the poor people and poor countries by introducing social businesses into the global framework.

Globalization can be a great force for good, one that can bring more benefits to the poor than any alternative. Global trade, for example, has played a major role in the economic growth of the past decade that has lifted millions of people out of poverty in China, India, and Bangladesh.

But it must be the right kind of globalization. The rule of "strongest takes all" must be replaced by rules that ensure that the poorest have a piece of the action, without being elbowed out by the richest. Globalization must not become financial imperialism.

Improved systems of national and international regulation of business are necessary and important. But to provide an alternative to the old-fashioned imperialist form of globalization, let's also use the creative potential of social business. In the years to come, powerful multinational social businesses can be created that will multiply the benefits of globalization for poor people and poor countries. Social businesses will bring ownership to the poor and keep profits within poor countries rather than draining them away to further enrich the wealthy. Building strong economies in the poor countries by protecting their national interest from plundering foreign companies will be a major area of interest for the social businesses of tomorrow.

Most important, our new international economic structure must build on the realization that we already have all the necessary tools to overcome our social problems.

At a glance, the most urgent problems in our world appear overwhelming, perhaps insoluble. But consider: Problems like hideous infectious diseases, rampant malnourishment, contaminated water supplies, lack of access to healthcare and education—all have been solved somewhere in our world. In fact, hundreds of millions of people take the solutions for granted. You, my reader, may be among them. The relatively privileged lives so many of us enjoy offer powerful proof that we *know* how to provide good education and healthcare; we *know* how to provide pure drinking water and healthful foods; we *know* how to cure or prevent most of the diseases that afflict the world's poor.

What's more, the tools for extending those solutions to every nation on Earth are readily available. Pharmaceutical companies hold patents for countless drugs that have the potential to help millions of people. Technology companies have IT and communications tools that could transform the lives of the world's poorest people. The agricultural experts of the world's great universities and research labs have techniques that could easily produce plenty of food for all. And even the economic resources are available, if we choose to use them wisely. In combination, the rich nations of the world give out over $60 billion each year as foreign aid to fight poverty. The problem is not lack of resources—it's the failure of our economic system to make those accessible to the people who need them most. Social business can make them accessible.

Everyone has a strong selfless impulse—a desire to help others that is just as powerful as the desire for personal gain. But traditional capitalism has never cared to make use of this strong urge in human beings. As a result, the world economy has continued to grow in a lopsided way, and the imbalance becomes worse as it grows.

Imagine a world without poverty, a world in which the imbalance has been corrected. Not only will it be a much better world for those who used to be poor, but everyone else will benefit, too. The economy will hit incredible new heights, as the market size for every product will double and triple. When everyone has access to excellent healthcare, the demand for highly trained doctors and nurses will skyrocket. When everyone can afford a nice house, construction companies and architects and furniture makers will be working overtime. Government expenditures on welfare programs will be unnecessary.

Everyone on this planet suffers personally when anyone's life is wasted. After all, the life that is wasted might have the potential to grow up and become the doctor who saves the life of my own grandchild, or the scientist who invents a device that will save the planet from global warming, or the artist who creates a magnificent work of art that will enrich my old age. Why should we waste that opportunity?

Some people seem to believe that if there are rich people, there have to be poor people. This is an outdated and inaccurate idea. It assumes that the rich get rich by taking away from the poor. It assumes that the total pie of wealth is of fixed size. If a few powerful people take away a big slice, the mass of people must end up with very little.

In reality, the economy is—or should be—an ever-growing pie. The rich can get richer and the poor can get less poor at the same time; there is no conflict. It is a question of the conceptual framework within which we view the economy. The present framework, which imagines an economy operated by one-dimensional human beings, gives enormous power and incentive to the rich to accumulate wealth without limit. That framework provides only one measure of success—the amount of money one possesses.

In a world of multi-dimensional people, everything changes. In this framework, success will be measured primarily by the contribution one makes to the well-being of the world.

To reduce the misery of poverty, we traditionally resort to the redistribution of income, taxing the rich and making the proceeds available to help the poor. In an economy populated by multi-dimensional people, a self-induced redistribution will take place when the rich undertake social businesses to eradicate social problems. Governments may find it easier and more effective to give incentives to the rich to solve social problems through their own initiatives by undertaking many kinds of social businesses, rather than using tax revenues just to run safety net and other inefficient public service programs.

In order to ensure that the poor benefit from economic growth, we need to ensure not only that the pie grows but also that the portion of the pie that goes to the poor grows even faster. Many argue that in a world of two types of businesses, growth will slow down because social businesses are not intended to produce large surpluses. I don't see this as a valid argument. When large numbers of people come out of poverty thanks to the successful operation of social businesses, profit-making companies will have larger markets and increased profits, while more people will have the capacity to consume and save. This will fuel the economy and help the poor move gradually into the world of the middle class.

In a world of one-dimensional people, the natural workings of the free market do not address social problems at all. Instead, the free market has a built-in tendency to create social and environmental problems. It's true that overall economic growth can ultimately benefit poor people. But the trickle-down effect that business-as-usual can have on poverty is an unreliable and agonizingly slow process. When the economic system creates barriers that reduce the opportunities available to the poor, as today's system does, then income disparities actually increase rather than shrink, since the pie grows faster on the rich people's side than it does on the poor people's side.

Social business has the potential to reverse this disparity because it addresses the poor directly and deliberately. By bringing the poor into the mainstream economic system, it helps their piece of the pie to grow independently.

Social business must be an essential part of the growth formula because it benefits the mass of people who would otherwise be disengaged. And when people are energized, so is the economy. Through access to credit, improved health services, better nutrition, high-quality education, and modern information technology, poor people will become more productive. They will earn more, spend more, and save more—to the benefit of everyone, rich and poor alike.

Social business can transform society very quickly because it will apply the amazingly powerful, rapidly-growing power of technology to improving the conditions of the poor and the environment. It will also liberate and harness the power of creativity, the sense of commitment of the new generation of young people of this new century, and the power of selflessness which defies all previous notions of human behavior in the economic world.

A Door to a New World

What will the world be like twenty or fifty years from now? It's fascinating to speculate. But I think an even more important question is: What *do we want* the world to be like twenty years or fifty years from today?

The difference has great significance. In the first formulation, we see ourselves as passive viewers of unfolding events. In the second, we see ourselves as active creators of a desired outcome.

I think it is time to take charge of our future rather than accept it passively. We spend too much time and talent predicting the future, and not enough on imagining the future that we would love to see. And even so, we don't do a very good job of predicting the future. With all our wisdom, expertise, and experience, we repeatedly fail to imagine the amazing changes that history continues to throw our way.

Think back to the forties. Nobody then predicted that within fifty years Europe would become a borderless political entity with a single currency. Nobody predicted that the Berlin Wall would fall, even a day before it happened. Nobody predicted that the Soviet Union would disintegrate and that so many independent countries would emerge out of it so quickly.

On the technology front, we see the same thing. In the sixties, no one predicted that a global network of computers called the Internet would soon take the world by storm. No one predicted that laptops, palm-tops, BlackBerrys, iPods, iPhones, and Kindles would be in the hands of millions. Even twenty years ago, no one was predicting that mobile phones would become an integral part of life in every village of the world.

Let's admit it: We could not have predicted the world of 2010 even from 1990—a span of only twenty years. Does this give us any credibility in predicting the world of 2030 today, given that each day the speed of change in the world gets faster and faster?

If we have to make predictions, there are probably two ways to go about it. One would be to invite the best scientific, technical, and economic analysts in the world to make their smartest twenty-year projections. Another would be to ask the world's most brilliant science-fiction writers to imagine the world of 2030. If you ask me who has the best chance of coming closer to the reality of 2030, without pausing for a second I'd say that the science-fiction writers would be far closer than the expert analysts.

The reason is very simple. Experts are trained to make forecasts on the basis of the past and present, but events in the real world are driven by the dreams of people.

We can describe the world of 2030 by preparing a wish list to describe the kind of world we would like to create by 2030. It might include:

- A world without a single person living in poverty
- A world whose oceans, lakes, streams, and atmosphere are free of pollution
- A world where no child goes to sleep hungry
- A world where no one dies a premature death from an avoidable illness
- A world where wars are a thing of the past
- A world where people can travel freely across borders
- A world where no one is illiterate and everyone has easy access to education through the application of new miracle technology
- A world where the riches of global culture are available to all

You can probably add dozens of beautiful wishes of your own. Whatever your personal wish list contains, that's what you should prepare for.

Dreams are made out of impossibles. We cannot reach the impossibles by using the analytical minds trained to deal with hard information that is currently available. These minds are fitted with flashing red lights to warn us about obstacles we may face. We'll have to put our minds in a different mode when we think about our future. We'll have to dare to make bold leaps to make the impossibles possible. As soon as one impossible becomes possible, it shakes up the structure and creates a domino effect, preparing the ground for making many other impossibles possible.

We'll have to believe in our wish list if we hope to make it come true. We'll have to create appropriate concepts, institutions, technologies, and policies to achieve our goals. The more impossible the goals look, the more exciting the task becomes.

Fortunately for us, we have entered into an age when dreams have the best chance of coming true. We must organize the present to allow an easy entry to the future of our dreams. We must not let our past stand in the way.

Do our dreams sound impossible? If they do, that means they are likely to come true if we believe in them and work for them. That's what the past fifty years have taught us.

So let's agree to believe in these dreams, and dedicate ourselves to making these impossibles possible.

If you are willing to share these dreams with me—and to join the people around the world who are already beginning to transform their dreams into reality through social businesses—let's undertake this exciting journey together.

INDEX

INDEX

[Photo credit: Tim Campbell]

Muhammad Yunus was born in Chittagong, Bangladesh, educated at Dhaka University, was awarded a Fulbright scholarship to study economics at Vanderbilt University, and became head of the economics department at Chittagong University in 1972. He is the founder and managing director of Grameen Bank. Yunus and Grameen Bank are winners of the 2006 Nobel Peace Prize. **Karl Weber** is a writer based in Irvington, New York. He co-authored Yunus's best-selling book, *Creating a World Without Poverty*.

PublicAffairs is a publishing house founded in 1997. It is a tribute to the standards, values, and flair of three persons who have served as mentors to countless reporters, writers, editors, and book people of all kinds, including me.

I. F. STONE, proprietor of *I. F. Stone's Weekly*, combined a commitment to the First Amendment with entrepreneurial zeal and reporting skill and became one of the great independent journalists in American history. At the age of eighty, Izzy published *The Trial of Socrates*, which was a national bestseller. He wrote the book after he taught himself ancient Greek.

BENJAMIN C. BRADLEE was for nearly thirty years the charismatic editorial leader of *The Washington Post*. It was Ben who gave the *Post* the range and courage to pursue such historic issues as Watergate. He supported his reporters with a tenacity that made them fearless and it is no accident that so many became authors of influential, best-selling books.

ROBERT L. BERNSTEIN, the chief executive of Random House for more than a quarter century, guided one of the nation's premier publishing houses. Bob was personally responsible for many books of political dissent and argument that challenged tyranny around the globe. He is also the founder and longtime chair of Human Rights Watch, one of the most respected human rights organizations in the world.

· · ·

For fifty years, the banner of Public Affairs Press was carried by its owner Morris B. Schnapper, who published Gandhi, Nasser, Toynbee, Truman, and about 1,500 other authors. In 1983, Schnapper was described by *The Washington Post* as "a redoubtable gadfly." His legacy will endure in the books to come.

Peter Osnos, *Founder and Editor-at-Large*